Becoming the Pastor You Hope to Be

Becoming the Pastor You Hope to Be

FOUR PRACTICES FOR IMPROVING MINISTRY

Barbara J. Blodgett

ALBAN

Herndon, Virginia
www.alban.org

The Alban Institute
2121 Cooperative Way, Suite 100
Herndon, VA 20171

Unless otherwise noted, all Scripture quotations are from the New Revised Standard Version of the Bible, © 1989, Division of Christian Education of the National Council of Churches of Christ in the United States of America, and are used by permission.

Cover design by Tobias Becker, Bird Box Design.

Library of Congress Cataloging-in-Publication Data

Blodgett, Barbara J., 1961-
  Becoming the pastor you hope to be : four practices for improving ministry / Barbara J. Blodgett.
     p. cm.
  Includes bibliographical references.
  ISBN 978-1-56699-411-8
  1. Pastoral theology. I. Alban Institute. II. Title.
  BV4011.3.B66 2011
  253--dc22
                              2011003900

11   12   13   14   15   VP   5   4   3   2   1

Contents

Foreword

IN DESCRIBING HIS MISSION, Jesus affirmed "I have come that they may have life, and have it abundantly" (John 10:10). These words were addressed to Jesus's first-century followers, but they are also addressed to us today. This quest is at the heart of Barbara Blodgett's *Becoming the Pastor You Hope to Be.* Barbara asserts that "ministerial formation must be founded on a commitment to excellence." This excellence is not accidental but involves a creative synthesis of grace and intentionality, and call and response. God is constantly calling to us through the events of our lives, but the quality of our lives and ministries depends on our self-awareness and response to God's call.

In the course of nearly twenty years of working in the area of professional spirituality and well-being, I often ask lawyers, doctors, and ministers, "Will you be glad you entered this profession twenty years from now? Will you still have joy in your professional life?" I then follow with a further question, "Will your closest friends, family, children, spouses, and partners also be grateful that you entered this profession?" The answers I receive often reveal the challenges of maintaining personal, professional, and relational wholeness.

Ministry, as Barbara Blodgett notes, can be a difficult and challenging profession, especially with its many and varied demands, the tendency toward isolation, and unrealistic expectations both by laypeople and pastors themselves. But, it can also be constantly rewarding and life-transforming. While God is always at work in the world—and in our congregations and lives as pastors—our intentionality opens us to greater manifestations of God's energy and power in our lives. When pastors practice the presence of God in their ministries, the routine and ordinary tasks of ministry can become windows of divine inspiration and healing.

Pastors can remain fresh and vital in ministry by continually nurturing and growing in their experience of the call that initially led them into ministry in the first place. This wisdom is as old as the apostle Paul's counsel to the Christians at Philippi: "I am confident of this, that the one who began a good work among you will bring it to completion by the day of Jesus Christ. . . . having produced the harvest of righteousness that comes through Jesus Christ for the glory and praise of God" (Phil. 1:3, 11) God is doing a good work in our lives and communities and we can become God's partners in ministry in our time and place, seeking faithful excellence in embodying God's call in our lives.

The apostle Paul also provides practices to enable us to produce a harvest of righteousness in Phil. 4:4–9. These practices involve gentleness, prayer, intercession, thanksgiving, joyfulness, and giving our attention to whatever is true, noble, honorable, and pure. With the apostle Paul, Barbara Blodgett notes that flourishing in ministry is the product of certain practices and behaviors, both personal and communal.

Our call as pastors is dynamic and many-faceted, whether or not we choose to be intentional. But, intentionality in terms of spiritual and professional growth and commitment to excellence ensures that our ministries continue to evolve in new and creative ways.

This journey toward wholeness in ministry is both a private and communal process. While pastors need to be persons of prayer, taking time for sabbath, daily contemplation, scripture study, and retreat, they also need the companionship of other professionals. It takes a village of supporting and caring colleagues to nurture a pastor. Faithful excellence in ministry, as Barbara Blodgett maintains, involves a number of simple, but transformative relational practices: caring but specific feedback, healthy and creative mentoring, and ongoing colleague groups aimed at professional support, study, and enrichment.

Ministry is a truly holy adventure of companionship with God and when we tend to our spiritual lives, relationships, and professional growth, our ministries will grow, flourish, and produce a harvest of righteousness.

Bruce G. Epperly
Epiphany 2011

Acknowledgments

WRITING THIS BOOK was the result of many years of collaborative work and thus serves as an example of the very topics it addresses. I am indebted to many colleagues and mentors who have taught me how to be a minister and how one learns to be one. To the interns, supervisors, Practicum teachers, and staff of the supervised ministry programs at Yale Divinity School from 1998 to 2008: you may discover yourselves in these pages! I hope I have represented you faithfully. Thank you. I also offer thanks to Stephen Arbogast, Lee Carroll, David Carter, and Pat Speer, who read and commented on chapters; to David Jenkins and Alice Rogers, who gave me opportunities to test out my critique of praise; to Noelle Damico, who helped me clarify my thoughts about excellence; to Dick Sparrow, who supported me in writing the book; and to my editor, Beth Gaede, whose interest in its ideas—and love of excellent sentences—sustained my own.

Throughout the book I have disguised identifying features of individuals whose stories I tell. Some stories and individuals are composites.

Introduction

MINISTERIAL FORMATION must be founded on a commitment to excellence. I believe all ministers are called to contribute to their ongoing formation by continually improving at what they do. I also believe that they grow and flourish, and even become happier in ministry, if they strive for excellence. Therefore this book urges clergy readers to develop practices that will help them become more excellent ministers. I do not mean "excellence" in the sense of excelling over others. The ministry is not a competition in which some must be left behind as others strive ahead. Nor is excellence the same as perfection. Many if not all practitioners can display excellence in what they do, while perfection is a rating reserved for only a flawless performance. You can do an imperfect job excellently. There is also more than one standard by which to measure excellence in a ministerial career. Certainly, I do not believe that bigger and higher are better and that becoming senior pastor of a "tall steeple church" or tenured professor or executive director of a large multistaff organization is every reader's aim. But ministers should give the best they can to their calling, whether they have been called to a small church or a cathedral or somewhere in between. My interest is in how *all* ministers can flourish. I assume that like me, readers want to set their sights high, not settling for mediocrity or disappointment in their vocation, and are willing to put some effort into forming themselves into the ministers they hope to become.

I have a friend who once claimed to live by the motto "If something's worth doing, it's worth doing mediocre." In other words, a moderately good job suffices if the end is really important. There is something to her philosophy. If we undertook only those things we could always do excellently, we might not undertake very much. Some things are important enough to do even if we cannot give them our very best. An adequate performance is good enough; at least we get something achieved. However, this philosophy can be dangerous, because it can seduce us into settling for that which is merely sufficient. My friend always pushes herself to attempt new endeavors that are worth her extra energy. Many of us, I fear, would instead content ourselves by neither attempting very much nor attempting to do things very well. I believe it is generally better to live by the motto that if something is worth doing, it is worth doing well. I unapologetically ask readers not to be content with doing a merely adequate job in ministry. Biblical scholar and theologian Walter Brueggemann has argued that ministers must adopt a mindset whereby "effective performance in ministry is not cause for congratulations, but it is normal, routine, and expected."[1] Only truly exceptional ministry should be cause for congratulations, while effective ministry done well should become the norm.

The vitality of our congregations may depend on adopting such a mindset. I believe one of the reasons why people become disenchanted with religion is that they encounter too much ineffective ministry. When people regularly experience congregational leadership done poorly or even just adequately, they begin to wonder whether merely adequate ministry is "routine and expected" by the church. By contrast, effective congregations are led by effective ministers, and those who joyously commit themselves to doing better work and learning to be better leaders tend to see an effect upon their congregations. Research has now shown, for example, that pastors who belong to peer groups are also pastors whose churches are growing. Other research shows that pastors who have mentors that empower them and teach them new things are more effective and struggle less to keep their congregations alive.

Why do those of us who lead congregations settle for less than excellence? People in general too often cast excellence as the idiosyncratic achievement of extraordinary individuals. Thus many of us think only a few who are especially blessed will excel. I am reminded of social scientist Malcolm Gladwell's work on what he called *outliers*, a term borrowed from statisticians to describe exceptional individuals who seem to break the mold and become supersuccessful in their fields. Gladwell argued that we too often ignore important reasons some people become excellent at what they do, because we tend to focus on how exceptionally talented and hardworking they must be. Outstanding individuals, he contended, *do* display talent and a penchant for hard work, but looking carefully, one can see that many *other* factors also contribute to their success. If you trace back through the stories of outliers, it turns out that you see not only genius but also remarkably consistent evidence of encouraging parents, teachers, and mentors; generous opportunities for practice and experimentation; ample access to resources; the right guidance and enculturation; and sometimes just the good luck of being in the right place at the right time. These factors provide as convincing an explanation for the excellence we see as does their seeming star power. As Gladwell argues,

The lesson here is simple. But it is striking how often it is overlooked. We are so caught in the myths of the best and the brightest and the self-made that we think outliers spring naturally from the earth. We look at the young Bill Gates and marvel that our world allowed that thirteen-year-old to become a fabulously successful entrepreneur. But that's the wrong lesson. Our world only allowed one thirteen-year-old unlimited access to a time-sharing terminal in 1968. If a million teenagers had been given the same opportunity, how many more Microsofts would we have today? To build a better world we need to replace the patchwork of lucky breaks and arbitrary advantages that today determine success . . . with a society that provides opportunities for all.[2]

In the ministry, the myth of excellence centers on identifying "the best and the brightest" candidates to ordain to the priesthood or pastorate. I have watched as significant resources are devoted to ferreting out those individuals who already show signs of having what it takes to be the best and listened as arguments are made for being more selective about who goes into ministry. I am not arguing that selectivity is wrong and that anyone can be a minister. Neither am I arguing against natural variation of gifts among people of faith. "Now there are varieties of gifts," wisely affirmed the apostle Paul. But it seems to me that we do ourselves and the whole church a disservice when we concentrate on fingering the few with talent rather than expanding opportunity for all. Why not devote resources to creating rigorous programs of education and formation for as *many* future church leaders as possible so that more of them can be excellent? Why not ask how we might *better* equip those already in leadership, throughout all stages of their careers, so that a better church can be built? Then, successful ministry would not be a matter of arbitrary advantage for only a few. It would become everyone's goal. After all, Paul also wrote that the body of Christ needs everybody and that we are to build each other up. He said that we cannot lift up only those parts of the body that are already most glorified.

Years ago a colleague of mine, seeing that I was dubious about the relationship between talent and excellence, pointed me to the work of a sociologist who had embedded himself in the world of competitive swimming in order to study routes to success across vocations. Daniel Chambliss found the world of swimming useful because it was so clearly stratified: the local country club league was nothing like regional competition, which was itself different from the nationals, and so on, up to Olympic class swimming. Therefore, it was relatively easy to identify the changes that individual swimmers had to make in order to progress from one level to the next. Improvement in swimming could be attributed to certain discrete factors. In a manner similar to Gladwell, Chambliss argued that mere talent is an insufficient explanation for why some swimmers make it to the top and others don't. "Talent," he said, is simply the term we use after the fact to try to make sense of an exemplary performance or a successful career. We don't see everything that goes into the making of great individuals, so we assign a mystery ingredient to them. "Great athletes, we seem to believe, are born with a special gift, almost a 'thing' inside of them, denied to the rest of us—perhaps physical, genetic, psychological, or physiological. Some have 'it,' and some don't. . . . We believe it is that talent, conceived as a substance behind the surface reality of performance, which finally distinguishes the best among our athletes."[3]

In short, we make mistakes about attribution. We attribute excellence either to "talent" or to other natural endowments and believe that only certain individuals possess them. I have often heard seasoned pastors say, about novices preparing for the ministry, that either they have "it" or they don't. But this logic would lead to the conclusion that only some are predestined to do ministry excellently. One would have to believe that the rest cannot really get any better. Seasoned pastors might object to my drawing such conclusions, protesting that they are merely observing how some individuals seem gifted in ways that no training or teaching can explain. They would call it the mystery of the Holy Spirit. Certainly, I acknowledge that the Spirit works in mysterious ways to bestow gifts on the people of God and does not always act democratically to make all people the same. But to acknowledge this is precisely to acknowledge that the movement of the Holy Spirit is not attributable to us! Our gifts are not ultimately our own to take credit for. But we can take credit—and responsibility—for what we do with them.

So what *does* lead to excellence or success in ministry, if not rare, inborn traits? A number of answers could probably be identified, including opportunity, dedication, competency, wisdom, passion, and luck. But in this book I am most interested first in the efforts ministers put into improving their practice, and second in their reliance on others who can teach them. Therefore, this book will look at several formative practices that ministers can and should adopt. All increase a minister's chances of doing well and flourishing and are especially effective if undertaken with others in community.

The first chapter shows you how to improve your skills by learning to solicit feedback from others. It explains the difference between praise and feedback and argues that praise can sometimes actually be detrimental to your growth and development. The second chapter encourages you to seek the company of mentors and use them well. Good mentors raise the bar for you and support you by taking a sustained interest in who you become. The third and fourth chapters outline the theory and practice, respectively, of peer groups. Peer groups are communities of learning created for the purpose of thinking with your colleagues about the work that you share and how to do it well. The fifth chapter shows how to examine your role in one particular realm of ministry, that of public life. It looks at choices you will face when you decide to get involved in public life: how to direct your efforts, how pragmatic to become, and to what extent you can share power.

Soliciting feedback, finding a mentor, belonging to a peer group, and examining your role may seem like simple and ordinary steps toward the goal of excellent ministry. But that's my point. Excellence is a matter of doing simple things with care and consistency. It is not magic. Improvement in ministry (as in other endeavors) comes about not through extraordinary leaps and bounds but rather through intentionally adopting simple habits and committing to carrying through on small but thoughtfully made choices. Daniel Chambliss listened to the way Olympic champions explained their success and was struck by how often they credited the seemingly slightest changes—showing up for practice on time, executing their turns differently. One key to their success was the belief that the little things really counted. As one of them put it, "People don't know how ordinary success is."[4] In the end, Chambliss concluded that "excellence is accomplished through the doing of actions, ordinary in themselves, performed consistently and carefully, habitualized, compounded together, added up over time."[5] I have chosen several practices that clergy can adopt, all ordinary in themselves, but which when undertaken with care and consistency can make a significant difference. In the chapters that follow, I will show you how and why these particular practices serve as a foundation for excellence in ministry.

Are You Daniel or King Belshazzar? Soliciting Feedback Instead of Praise

AS PASTORS, I BELIEVE, we are made not born.[1] Therefore we need others around us who are committed to helping make us into the pastors we will become. We need them at all stages of our vocation. Seasoned as well as new pastors need people to talk with on a regular basis about what constitutes excellent ministry practice. We all need feedback on how we are doing if we are going to learn new skills and hone old ones. Otherwise we stumble around attempting to improve our practice through guesswork or trial and error. Unfortunately, one of the common features of the way a ministry career unfolds is that regular, on-going assessment tends to disappear after our credentials are established. Pastors are not always required to continue training after they are authorized for ministry, and therefore they do not receive the same kind of formal evaluation they did in school. New pastors in particular sometimes find that while they do not necessarily wish to be graded anymore, they do wish they still could receive some feedback, if only to figure out how the skills they learned apply to their new context. As pastor and professor of ministry M. Craig Barnes writes in an essay on his own transition from seminary to parish, "Maybe it's out of necessity, or perhaps just tradition, but we prepare people for ministry through highly structured, clearly graded, and easily evaluated programs of study. The goals are clear and so are the expectations that have to be met in order to make progress toward those goals. All this objective evaluation seemed stressful to me when I was a student, but I yearned for it after I became a young pastor who was no longer sure what progress even meant."[2] Whether or not your own experience of theological education was one of clear goals and expectations, Barnes's point is nevertheless well taken. In contrast to the formal preparation leading up to professional ministry, the actual doing of ministry itself is far less structured and its goals less transparent. You might sometimes feel at a loss knowing exactly what you should be doing and what the yardstick will be for assessing your success once you do figure it out.

This is not to say that the ministry lacks any process of evaluation; indeed, parishioners are often quick to judge their pastors. But their evaluation frequently takes a very informal and implicit form. When pastors do receive feedback, moreover, it too often manifests itself in one of two less-than-helpful ways: either unreflective criticism or generalized praise. This chapter takes a close look at praise in particular and suggests an alternative.

A Biblical Metaphor

Praise receives widespread endorsement in North American culture as a form of motivation and encouragement. Faith communities in particular are especially prone to praising their clergy out of a genuine desire to be supportive. But praise can seduce us and even become dangerous for us. Let us begin with a biblical metaphor that demonstrates the seductive power of praise. In the fifth chapter of the book of Daniel, we hear the story of the court servant Daniel being summoned by King Belshazzar to decipher and interpret a mysterious writing that has appeared on the wall of the royal palace. Daniel, of course, is an exile from Judah who had been brought into the king's court by King Belshazzar's father, King Nebuchadnezzar. Daniel's reputation for intelligence and knack for interpretation precedes him, so this is why he has been summoned for this particular task. King Belshazzar is unnerved by the mysterious inscription on the wall. The biblical text does not tell us quite what is so unnerving, but for Belshazzar it may be his own illiteracy. The king lacks the ability to read the words, let alone interpret them. He may feel a bit upstaged by Daniel. Therefore when his queen urges him to solicit Daniel's help, he does, though doing so wounds his pride a bit.

Perhaps because of his insecurity, or his pride, King Belshazzar uses his position of power to offer Daniel three rewards for interpreting the writing: "You shall be clothed in purple," he tells Daniel, "have a chain of gold around your neck, and rank third in the kingdom" (5:16). But Daniel rebuffs the king's tokens. This is my favorite moment in the story. He tells the king, "Let your gifts be for yourself, or give your rewards to someone else! Nevertheless I will read the writing to the king and let him know the interpretation" (5:17). The prophet does agree to offer his skills at interpretation, but he will do so for his own reasons and on his own terms. He will reject the bribery implied in the proffered tokens of imperial power.

The story concludes with Daniel reading the inscription with ease. He interprets the words on the wall, which deliver a scathing indictment of King Belshazzar and a warning to him. That night the king is killed and a new king ascends to the throne.

But let us return to the moment in the story when Daniel rejects the king's rewards, for I suspect there is a message here about courage and resistance and, ultimately, about rewards like praise. It would have been so easy for Daniel to give in to the seduction of power and prestige represented by being asked to assist the king. And yet by not letting himself be flattered, Daniel claimed a measure of freedom from his enslavement by the royal court and its powers and principalities. Therefore, to me the moment is metaphor for resisting rewards. Praise is one kind of reward that is all too easily bestowed and all too happily received but might better be resisted. Many times praise is lavished on others by praise givers who do so from a position of power (like the king) in order to exercise it. Stroking someone else's ego, after all, is a way of stroking one's own. Other times praise is simply offered out of habit. The notion that performance should be rewarded with praise is well accepted. No matter the reason it gets overused, however, praise is not the "magic bullet" it is cracked up to be. It does not always succeed in getting people to do better or to be happier. That is why I admire the rare Daniels of the world who seem indifferent to praise. They seem to know something the rest of us don't about its hidden dangers.

People receive many kinds of rewards in life, often for doing what they would have done anyway, like Daniel exercising his skill of interpretation. Think of Employee of the Month awards, class rankings, gifts for years of service at jobs, gold stars for good behavior. Once when I was in elementary school, I received free tickets to a Cleveland Indians baseball game at the end of the year for getting straight As. Now, I won't deny that it was fun to go to the game and see the congratulatory announcement light up the scoreboard, but I remember being rather mystified by all the fuss. From my perspective, all I had done was go to school and do my work. And I do *not* remember that getting to go to the game made me (or any of my classmates, for that matter) work any harder the next year.

Praise is one of those rewards. Not only is it sometimes a symbol of power but, more important, it is also often superfluous, unnecessary, and even uninspiring. I believe that praising people—that is, lauding them for attributes like their intelligence, natural ability, artistry, and so on—does not necessarily motivate them to do better and may even have negative consequences. While most of us accept the idea that we shouldn't label people for their shortcomings—in theological terms, we should hate the sin but not the sinner—many of us still seem to insist upon labeling people for their natural abilities and qualities. Sometimes we call these their *gifts*. But why should this be? Why not "love not the gifted one but the giving itself"? And so my counsel would be *not* to tell a new minister, "You're just the greatest preacher" or "You're a natural born pastor," but to talk about the preaching or the pastoring instead. The latter would be called giving feedback rather than praise.

Praise versus Feedback

I hasten to clarify the distinction between praise and feedback, as I am using these terms. *Praise* is simply a blanket summary statement of how good someone is, without explaining what in particular they are good at and what is good about it. (Some would call this empty praise.) It consists of unspecific laudatory comments directed toward persons qua persons; that is, toward their attributes or their identity rather than their behavior or performance. "You're a math genius." "You're such a gifted singer." "You have a pastor's heart." "You've inherited your daddy's artistic gene." (A friend of mine supplied this last one, and then guiltily acknowledged to me that her *other* daughter—the one supposedly lacking the artistic gene—now avoids anything having to do with art.) *Feedback*, in contrast, consists of statements about the nature of what someone did. It is directed not toward a person's attributes but toward their actions. So, for instance, "I admire the work you did to get a ninety-eight on that math quiz" is an example of feedback rather than praise. "Your singing makes me feel so serene." "I can tell that you brought comfort to that grieving family." "Tell me about choosing those vivid colors for your paintings." Note that feedback can be just as positive and approving; it simply shifts the focus away from a person's identity and onto the effort and engagement they put into the task.

By differentiating between praise and feedback, I am not differentiating between positive and negative. It is not that praise consists of positive statements and feedback of negative ones, because feedback can be either positive or negative. (And praise has an opposite, which we might call *unreflective criticism*—a blanket statement of how bad someone is.) Apparently, some educators do not believe in positive statements of any kind. I once heard of a student who spent an entire summer in an instructional program under a supervisor who refused to say anything positive about her work, even when she specifically asked him for positive feedback so she might know when she was getting it right. Instead, he reportedly told her that she needed to develop her own internal sense of her work and her own positive feelings toward it rather than rely on him. Now, this supervisor may be onto something, but I do not happen to subscribe to his educational philosophy. I have always believed people learn from their successes as well as their failures, and that they sometimes need help from others to identify both; therefore, detailing the positive aspects of what someone has done is a valuable practice.

I have discovered over the years that pointing out the dangers of praise does not make me very popular. After all, who among us does not like being praised? It feels good. It feels like a natural conclusion to a job well done. We also like giving praise. Offering it feels good and comes naturally. In fact many of us are quite committed to the idea that we can inspire others to higher levels of learning and achievement by praising them. We are like King Belshazzar when it comes to assuming that praise should naturally accompany our efforts to get people to do what we want them to do. In addition, we tend to think that if someone we are mentoring lacks the necessary confidence to perform better, our praise will supply it. Finally, we assume that without praise novices might never discover their gifts. I am doubtful of all of these claims (that praise motivates, increases confidence, and aids discernment). It's not at all clear to me that people would not work just as hard, perform just as highly, and know what they are good at without our laudatory comments.

The Danger of Praise

It turns out that, as unpopular as they might be, I am not alone in my hunches about praise. Researchers who have actually studied it have demonstrated that people work just as hard, perform just as highly, and know what they are good at without praise. In fact, as it turns out, they often do even better without it.

Chief among the educators and scholars who have researched praise and feedback is social psychologist Carol Dweck, formerly of Columbia University and now at Stanford. Dweck believes that success of many kinds—excelling in sports, succeeding in business, doing well in school—is ultimately aided not by boosting people's sense of their natural abilities or attributes but rather by boosting their engagement in and passion for their endeavors. When it comes to academic achievement, for example, a student is better off believing in their effort than their intelligence.

Dweck's most famous studies were conducted in fifth grade classrooms across different regions of the United States, involving four hundred students in all. First, her researchers gave students a set of nonverbal puzzles that were designed at only a moderate level of difficulty. They all completed the puzzles satisfactorily and afterward were told their scores. A control group heard only their scores. In a second group, students were praised for their intelligence. In addition to their scores they were told, "You must be smart at this." A third group of students were praised for their effort. Researchers said to them, "You must have worked really hard at this." Students in all three groups were then offered the following choice: If there were time remaining at the end of the session, they could work either on puzzles that weren't too hard so that they wouldn't get many wrong or on ones that they would learn a lot from, even if they wouldn't look so smart. Their choices were revealing. Far more students who had been praised for their intelligence chose to work on the easy puzzles than those who had been praised for their effort. In contrast, Dweck's data revealed that 90 percent of the fifth graders who had been told "You must have worked really hard" asked to work on difficult puzzles they would learn something from.

In a second phase of the same study, all of the fifth graders worked on puzzles designed at a seventh grade difficulty level, two levels above their own. All of them predictably performed less well; this trial was in effect an artificially induced failure. It was designed to discover what attributions students would make for their failure to solve the puzzles. When observed and questioned during this trial, students in the two initial groups responded quite differently: those in the "intelligence" group got visibly distressed and said things like "I guess I wasn't as smart after all," while those in the "effort" group did not appear discouraged and said things like "I guess I'm not working hard enough." Some in the latter group announced that it was their favorite test, suggesting that the hard work was welcome. A few even appeared to relish the challenge. Finally, all the students were given a third set of puzzles to work on, this one designed to be as easy as the first. Their scores resulted in a dramatic finding. Those children who had originally been praised for their intelligence consistently did worse on the third puzzle set than they had in the very beginning. Even though the puzzles in the third set were no more difficult than those in the first, these students performed worse on them.[3]

One line of praise actually lowered test scores. When interviewed later about her study, Carol Dweck said that she and her researchers had a hunch going in about the detrimental effects of praise, but even they were surprised that one simple comment would make such a difference. Since this study, Dweck has gone on to conduct a great deal more research on praise, among all sorts of people, and she has consistently found that praise has a deleterious effect on success. As she explains,

> After seven experiments with hundreds of children, we had some of the clearest findings I've ever seen: Praising children's intelligence harms their motivation and it harms their performance.
>
> How can that be? Don't children love to be praised?
>
> Yes, children love praise. And they especially love to be praised for their intelligence and talent. It really does give them a boost, a special glow—but only for the moment. The minute they hit a snag, their confidence goes out the window and their motivation hits rock bottom. If success means they're smart, then failure means they're dumb.[4]

Mindsets

Dweck believes that what she found in these fifth graders' experience of being tested is replicated in a pattern driving all of us. Some of us have what she calls a "fixed mindset" with respect to our capacities. We believe that our intelligence, athleticism, musical talent, and other attributes are fixed and given, that we either came into this world possessing them or not, and that there is little we can do to change that fact. Those of us who possess such a mindset find reinforcement in all the messages we receive from an early age telling us we are smart, talented, gifted, and so on. Others of us, on the other hand, believe that our capacity to excel can always be cultivated. Dweck calls this having a "growth mindset." According to the growth mindset, "everyone can change and grow through application and experience" and no one's potential can be known with certainty ahead of time.[5] The growth mindset pertains, incidentally, even to mindsets, believing not that they are fixed but rather that a person can change hers from fixed to growth.[6] It is detectable in the passion some people have for persisting at their projects and pushing themselves to improve, even and especially when they are not doing particularly well. Dweck says she *discovered* the growth mindset while watching kids who relished really hard problems and who, rather than being dismayed by the difficulty of the task, actually seemed spurred on by it. A growth mindset might be summarized by what one urban public school teacher I heard of constantly tells her students: "Smart is not something you are. It's something you work at."

A fixed mindset can be dangerous for those of us who have it, because it indisposes us to failure. If I am told my whole life that I am gifted, for quite a while I might do just fine—in part because I will carefully choose activities that guarantee my success and prove my giftedness, just like the fifth graders. But when the time comes that I fail at something—which is going to happen eventually—I will be not only disappointed but also *defeated*. I will be ill equipped to cope with my failure. I will be less likely to chalk it up to a bad day during which I did not do my best or to an ill-chosen strategy or to bad luck. And should it be the case that my failure is the result of someone else's prejudice or unfair treatment, I will not notice. I will not search for any of these reasons to explain my failure. I will simply paste the proverbial L to my forehead signifying that I think I must be a loser.[7]

Ordained ministry can be a stressful and even competitive realm where pastors measure themselves against each other and against deeply held ideas about who they are and what they are capable of. Whether they articulate it or not, many pastors who are starting their careers or starting in new positions ask themselves, "Will ministry come easily to me so that I will do well at it?" "Am I good at this?" and the theological cousin to such questions, "Am I called to this?" As a field educator, I had several moments over the years of being stricken to discover that students felt unworthy to become ministers and doubted their choice of ministerial study. Of course my impulse was to rush in and heap on the praise. But if pastors' insecurities are met this way, it may ironically be adding fuel to the fire.

What, therefore, should you as a pastor do? While I cannot necessarily take up the whole theory of mindsets and ways to develop one for growth, I can at least show what kind of feedback you need and how you can learn to solicit it. First, let me describe an experience I had trying to institute a practice of feedback in place of praise. This will not only help us further appreciate the seduction of praise but also suggest concrete ways for you to initiate a practice of feedback in your pastoral ministry.

An Experiment in Feedback

As the director of a divinity school internship program, I worked with pairs of student interns and their supervisors to create quality internship experiences where interns would grow in their pastoral skills and identity under the guidance and mentoring of experienced supervisors. Most internships were very rich, but I began to suspect that one thing that might improve the experience for students would be if they received more and better feedback at their sites. Interns were generally beloved by the communities where they were learning to practice ministry. They received a lot of praise for their work, which, not unsurprisingly, made them feel good. But their reports of their experience suggested that they were often left on their own to figure out a great deal about how to do ministry. They were given ample opportunities by their supervisors to practice new skills, like preaching and teaching and so forth, and generally were told they were doing fine—but something was still missing. Too many would arrive at their weekly reflection groups on campus still unsure about how and what they were doing. One way of putting it is that too often they were like swimmers who were thrown into the pool to sink or swim, and even when most of the time they swam just fine, they could not necessarily say why. These interns were like Barnes, the young pastor quoted earlier: they could use more opportunities to assess how they were doing and even to learn what constituted progress. I decided that interns needed more time built into their internships for reflecting on their performance and gaining wisdom about what made their ministry go well. In part, interns simply needed less praise and more feedback.

Hoping therefore to help wean intern-supervisor pairs off of praise and onto feedback, I designed a process called the Observation Report. Adapted from a technique I had learned years ago in training student teachers, it required supervisors to pay close attention to their interns while the interns were engaged in practicing ministry skills (the way master teachers observe student teachers in the classroom). It also invited interns to request the specific forms of feedback they would find most useful. One of my supervisors, a former athlete, said the Observation Report technique put him in mind of the way athletes in training get literal (physical) feedback from their muscles as well as observational feedback from their coaches, both of which let them know in a tangible way that they are improving at their sport. My hope was that the Observation Report would discipline both supervisors and interns in the giving and receiving of concrete and specific feedback. My theory was that the main reason supervisors praised their interns was not because they were King Belshazzars but simply because they didn't set aside enough time to offer feedback. A universal, blanket statement like "You're so great" makes up for that.[8]

The Observation Report was to be accomplished in three parts. First, the intern was to write down what skill they would be working on in the activity being observed, add something about their personal and professional goals relative to the particular skill, and say what it was they wanted their supervisor to watch for. Then, the supervisor would show up for the activity and observe the intern doing ministry. Finally, the supervisor was to answer the intern's questions and offer any additional feedback that was especially pertinent but for which the intern may not have asked.

I thought it would be so simple.

Instead, I noticed several kinds of resistance to the practice of feedback. Interestingly, one form of resistance seemed to come from the interns themselves. Some of them, when asked to write about their goals going into the activity to be observed, described such challenges as getting enough people to attend a program, having sufficient time for what they were hoping to do, or relying on volunteers to come through. In other words, things that were important to a successful activity but that would fall largely outside their control. It was as though they resisted hearing feedback on their part in the success of the ministry. Or perhaps they simply did not know how to identify their part and set their own goals.

Sometimes supervisors exacerbated this problem. They would respond to such requests for feedback by confirming the appropriateness of the concerns, saying things like "I never know myself who's going to show up." It was as if they were saying, "Yes, ministry is just really hard sometimes" and leaving it at that without identifying the nature of the difficulty or possible responses. Then, they would praise the intern with statements like "You were great, given the circumstances." I came to name this pattern on the part of interns and supervisors *collusion*, and I began to wonder: Do we like receiving praise for hard things as a substitute for analyzing what is hard about them? As praise givers, do we sometimes use praise to cover our own anxiety about the hard things we are asking others to do? Indeed, upon reflection, one supervisor admitted that praise was a way for him to mask the anxiety of "the intern inside him."

I noticed another pattern in the reports that suggested a second kind of resistance to feedback and a preference for praise. I found it very common for supervisors to comment on how "natural" their intern seemed at ministry. In other words, they regularly attributed success to the intern's qualities. They praised their intern for being natural in performing an activity even and especially when interns had explicitly stated their discomfort or trepidation with it. Clearly, those interns had not yet attributed any excellent performance to their "nature," yet supervisors seemed eager to do so. They very rarely attributed their interns' success to hard work or strategies of improvement. When supervisors did note improvement, they tended to make blanket statements like "She's come a long way in her preaching," without saying what that way was or how the intern came along it. I suspect that supervisors and others talk about *natural* abilities when they mean *excellent*, because often when something is done very well it looks smooth and effortless. However, if you think closely about it, when we go out of our way to praise people for what they do naturally or effortlessly, we are specifically disvaluing any effort they put in. People say, "He's good, but he had to work at it," as though working at something is an embarrassment. But why should we applaud success that was not earned through work?

Third, supervisors tended to resist my instructions to limit themselves when giving feedback to simply telling what they saw. Many tended to heap on adjectives; for example, "When I watched, I saw a mature, graceful, and devout teacher." "Marianne is a wonderful communicator—poised, clear, funny, and not afraid." "Shelly showed a natural gift for preaching—she *wants* to be in the pulpit." Overall, I found that supervisors' initial attempts at the Observation Report process tended toward generalization and flattery. Some tried to stick to feedback but could not help themselves and amended a concluding praise-worthy comment. Almost without exception, supervisors used the space for further comments not to add further pertinent observations but rather to make a summary statement like "Aaron has the potential to become an extraordinary preacher!" One supervisor wrote there, almost apologetically, "I don't want my comments about delivery to take away from the fact that overall Anne is a good, solid preacher." It is as though, like Carol Dweck's fifth graders, they felt a need to provide assurance that their intern was, in fact, a good one. I got the sense that many thought by not implicitly giving their intern a high score and producing a favorable comparison to other theoretical interns, they were responding inadequately. Or, perhaps, it was as though commenting on specific details as one does when giving feedback did not seem *enough*, so general comments ("good, solid preacher") were thrown in to round out the assessment.

Finally, some supervisors could not help but express personal satisfaction with their intern. They would go well beyond the activity observed to write about how proud they were of the intern's ministry or how grateful they were to get to work with that intern. To me, statements like these suggest that praise is often used to express two sentiments: pride and gratitude. Both pride and gratitude have their place, but they reflect more on the praise giver than the praised.

In the Observation Report process, supervisors were given the option of letting a layperson or a staff member do an occasional report. It was interesting to note during the first year that, without exception, such nonclergy individuals gave more straightforward assessments that avoided praise-laden language. For example, one parishioner wrote about listening to a sermon, "The message was quite clear to me; however, Chris does tend to rush a bit." They also provided more detail. In a mental health setting where the intern was running a program, a staff member observed, "I saw people genuinely interested in her presentation. The room was quiet with almost all eyes on the podium, which doesn't always happen here." I came to conclude that laypeople were generally free of the need to express how proud and grateful they were for the intern's performance—perhaps because they had less riding on the intern's success—and could just get on with the business of feedback.

Over the years, supervisors in my program did get better at providing the kind of feedback I had hoped for. And it was not because I praised them! We all worked hard together to perfect the practice of the Observation Report. Some continued to wonder why I was so insistent on it, and others raised legitimate and thoughtful questions about whether the specific reporting technique served its purpose, but most eventually agreed that, at the very least, the reports helped discipline them to have the kind of regular, ongoing conversation about the doing of ministry they knew their interns deserved.

Feedback for Pastors

There are obvious differences between feedback for pastors and feedback for the interns whose stories I have told. For one thing, pastors do not always have a supervisor to whom to turn. Those of you working solo, therefore, have to solicit feedback either from mentors outside the church or from lay leaders. Even those of you working as associates would benefit from soliciting feedback from people other than the senior pastor, for multiple sources of feedback are best and yours should not be limited only to your supervisory relationship. I will concentrate here on a process of seeking feedback from lay leaders rather than supervisors.

Second, while I would never discount the important contributions interns make to the settings where they work, the reality of internships is that they are designed for the benefit of interns and their learning. Students are allowed and even encouraged to design their work around their needs and goals. By this I mean that they are encouraged to experiment with new projects, are given the freedom to fail, and can choose to undertake ministry tasks on the basis of their educational value. A pastor's situation is a bit different. While you may be committed to learning from your work, you are expected to design ministry tasks around the needs and goals of your whole church. You are not as free to construct projects solely as a way to develop into a better minister. What this means is that the purpose of feedback for you shifts somewhat. In fact it can and should appropriately be folded into the larger process of evaluating your church's ministry, because it's not just about you.

Many pastors (especially new ones) are like interns, however, in that they often describe their experience as that of sink or swim. It can feel isolating and overwhelming to have to figure what the goals of the church are, how your tasks can meet those goals, and then how to make meaning afterward of what you tried to do. Being praised can temporarily make you feel competent and connected to others. And yet as gratifying as it may be to receive words of praise from the people in your congregation, it is even more helpful to receive thoughtful reflection, observation, and constructive critique from them. Ultimately, it is feedback that will boost your confidence, help you develop your pastoral abilities, and move you toward excellent ministry practice. Let me outline, therefore, steps in a process of soliciting feedback.

ADMIT YOUR DESIRE FOR PRAISE

Before even beginning a process of soliciting feedback, you would be wise to acknowledge that feedback will feel different from praise. It has a different emotional quality and may not initially feel as rewarding or satisfying. Desire for praise is deeply rooted in many of us. For some, especially those of us who grew up in an earlier era, praise was denied us as children. Parents of previous generations tended not to lavish praise on their children. (In part, they did not receive as many cultural messages telling them to offer rewards as a way of encouraging good behavior.) Consequently, the offspring of those generations may welcome hearing praise as adults and believe in its benefits. For others of us, receiving praise has been a way of life. It has accompanied every achievement we have ever gained. Having been told we are terrific from an early age on, we tend to hear in compliments proof of our self-worth. We, too, believe in the power of praise, albeit for different reasons.

Therefore, many of us crave hearing that our successes in ministry are due to our talent and giftedness. Especially for those of us with a fixed mindset, it affirms our sense of self to attribute any success we achieve to our natural qualities. Furthermore, I suspect that clergy may be particularly invested in the idea that pastoral abilities are fixed and given. After discovering the difference, described previously, between the way clergy and nonclergy observed their interns, I began to wonder whether clergy in contrast to laypeople may on the whole be more committed to the idea that ministers are born rather than made. Clergy do talk a great deal about discovering gifts and sometimes less about cultivating them. They can tend to associate giftedness with a call to ministry. Could it be that clergy cling to a fixed mindset about the gifts and callings of ministry because feeling gifted rewards us for labor that has few other rewards?

Or perhaps clergy are like many of today's parents who have a difficult time giving up on praise because of a legitimate desire to express love. Reporting on Carol Dweck's work, one writer, who was also a father, was inspired to switch the kind of praise he gave his son from general positive statements to specifics instead (such as praising his son's passing ability in soccer games). Chronicling his efforts in an article entitled "How *Not* to Talk to Your Kids: The Inverse Power of Praise," he writes of discovering the association he had made between *love* and praise, and admits that he had used praise as a way to express his love for his son. "Truth be told, while my son was getting along fine under the new praise regime, it was I who was suffering. It turns out that I was the real praise junkie in the family. . . . I recognized that praising him with the universal 'You're great—I'm proud of you' was a way I expressed unconditional love."[9] Indeed, clergy often object to my attempts to wean them off praise, saying that praising people is their *job*. Their role, they say, is to extend God's unconditional love to others, and now I am asking them to curtail this role. (My response is to affirm their expressions of love but to question whether love must always be demonstrated through praise.)

All this is to say that there are many different reasons why you as a pastor may feel that receiving feedback without all the "strokes" is less than completely satisfying. The kind of affirmations I am calling praise often get closely associated in the ministry with affirmations of call, support for one's gifts, and expressions of unconditional love. "You are a wonderful pastor" may seem to affirm you in a way that even "You preached a wonderful sermon this morning" may not. You may believe at some level that global, praiseworthy statements about who you are as a minister will affirm your calling. Therefore, it may be important to distinguish a desire for feedback from a desire to be approved and loved by those you serve. This will help you initiate a process of soliciting feedback.

INITIATE THE PROCESS

Many laypeople will share these same convictions about the value of praise. Unless they happen to be supervisors or educators by vocation who understand your need for feedback as a lifelong learner, few will likely initiate it for you. You will have to request it. You can do this in two ways.

First, and probably easiest, is to ask for details when somebody comments on something you did. This may not be feasible in all situations; asking everybody to be specific about what they liked in your sermon as you are shaking hands after church is neither possible nor appropriate. But if someone sends you an e-mail on Monday praising in general ways your sermon from the day before, you can reply with a question such as "What did you hear?" or even more simply, "What did you like about it?" It has become nearly second nature for me to respond to compliments about activities I lead with questions. To someone's comment "That was great!" I will reply, "Thank you! I'm glad. Can you tell me what you thought was great *about* it?" I have invariably found that people are not only able to supply more detail but also enjoy doing so. In many cases, they may have to pause to think first, but then they usually tell me something about what they experienced or took away from the activity. Sometimes they will be able to tell me something about my part—a choice I made, a particular thing I said, or a way I handled a situation. Both are great forms of feedback because either way I learn more about how my actions ministered to another person.

A second way to request feedback is to ask for it ahead of time. Before you are to lead in worship, preach a sermon, or teach a class, for example, invite a trusted individual or select set of individuals to pay special attention for you. Tell them what you would like them to watch for. Be as specific as you can. Simply saying "Tell me how I'm doing" or "Tell me how it went" will probably not suffice. They will likely respond either with flattery or with concerns of their own. Observers commonly use the observation process to voice their own idiosyncratic hopes, desires—and complaints—about your ministry in general. If you make your request for feedback a general one, you open the door for responses that have little to do with the task at hand. Voice your particular interests and concerns so as to direct your observers' attention toward them. For example, "I will be experimenting with preaching from the center aisle without notes, and I want to know whether this more casual style engages my listeners or just gives me license to ramble.'" "I am concerned that the boys in youth group don't feel comfortable talking since they are so outnumbered by the girls. Will you please watch how I respond to the boys when I lead discussion?" Even when you direct the feedback process this way you will receive extraneous comments; these may or may not prove helpful, but at least you have improved your chances of hearing what you want by requesting it ahead of time.[10]

Asking for feedback in advance has a secondary benefit, which is the way it focuses your own attention. Whenever you take the time to articulate your goals, whether simply for yourself or for others, you improve your chance of meeting them. Educators suggest goal setting not only because it's a way to become more efficient but also because the process draws your mind to the deeper purposes behind what you are doing. Chances are, for example, that the pastor who asks for feedback on preaching without notes will have thought through the reasons for attempting such a switch and the thought process in itself will, in fact, make him less inclined to ramble. This is not just because he knows someone is watching but also because he reflected ahead of time on the potential value of extemporaneous preaching; that value will surely be reflected in his practice. Approaching your practice with purpose is almost always better than making arbitrary choices. The real beauty of the process of soliciting feedback ahead of time, then, is the way it helps you become more intentional about your ministry. Others will enjoy collaborating with you in that intentional process.

PRESS FOR SPECIFICS

As I have argued, the difference between praise and feedback often comes down to the difference between generalities and specifics, as well as a difference between person-focused versus action-focused reflections. The latter require more work of your observers. We pastors need to train ourselves and others not to praise *us* but rather what we *do*. There is a subtle but important difference, for example, between being told "You really know your Bible" and "That was a great Bible study." And even better than "That was a great Bible study" is to be told "That was a great Bible study because you helped us connect the good Samaritan story to our own lives." When people direct their compliments to you as a person, try to invite them to rephrase. Should people try to set you up in comparison to other pastors, try to redirect them back to describing the ministry activity and what it meant to them.[11]

One of the best ways of asking for specific feedback is to ask observers to tell you what they see and hear. I often describe the role of observer as that of offering a second set of eyes and ears. The observer functions like the camera or recorder we play back after our performance to see what we *really* looked or sounded like. Caught up in the leadership of an activity, we cannot pay attention to everything at once. We have only our own perspective on how it is going, but ours is simply not the only view of our work. Neither is it necessarily the best nor most accurate. Details observed by someone with another perspective will often benefit us enormously because they lend an interpretation as well as mere facts. For example, someone observing your youth group might notice that while the boys do less of the talking during discussion, they do not appear to be shut down by the number of girls or their chattiness. Perhaps the boys' comments are few but significant, and this distinction had escaped you because you had equated silence with lack of engagement. In other words, observers function even better than a camera or recorder because they additionally help us make *meaning* out of our experiences.

Asking someone to be your eyes and ears is also a way to deflect the praise response. Someone asked to attend to details, like keeping track of how many youth talk during a discussion, will have their attention trained elsewhere. They are less likely afterward to give a summary statement such as "You are just so gifted with the youth." They are also less likely to give responses based on their own personal preferences.

ACCEPT NEGATIVE FEEDBACK, TOO

I should point out that although I have been giving examples only of positive feedback, the same process I have been describing applies to negative feedback. The corollary to praise, after all, is unreflective criticism. Negative feedback and unreflective criticism are not the same thing. The former can help us learn and grow by pointing out the specific reasons we may have failed to do our best. The latter is rarely helpful. "You're a lousy administrator" simply does not contain much useful information, whereas an administrator might be able to work with something like "You shoot from the hip too often in staff meetings so that the staff feels their ideas go unheard." We may never enjoy hearing negative feedback, but there are bound to be times when we minister less effectively than others, and at those times feedback is preferable to criticism.

It can become equally if not more important to deflect criticism in the ministry as it is to deflect praise. Just as with praise, people criticize others not so much intending to encourage their improvement but rather to express their own feelings and reactions. That is, criticism usually says more about the critic than the one being criticized. Keeping this in mind, however difficult it can be, will help you interpret what you are hearing. Criticism tells you more about the people you are ministering with and to. It clarifies for you what they value.

Putting criticism in perspective is important, as is attempting not to take it personally. Learning how to handle negativity well is crucial if only because of the human tendency to dwell on the worst responses to our endeavors. Nearly every minister

I have talked to about being evaluated agrees that the negative comments are the ones that stay with them. "I can hear a hundred comments about a worship service, with ninety nine of them being positive, but when I go home, it will be the one negative comment that I remember."

Therefore, it will help to practice the same strategies with criticism as I have outlined for praise. Try to turn it into feedback. Ask your critics for specifics. Initiate dialogue that will solicit helpful responses from them. Tell them that you would like to learn from their perceptions and experiences of your work. Invite them in a nondefensive manner to say more. Cultivate an attitude of receptivity to observations, both positive and negative. Be curious about their experience as a way of inspiring their curiosity about yours. Share your goals for your activities with them ahead of time and be transparent as you go along about the things you are doing to work toward your goals. Build time for feedback into as many different activities of ministry as possible so that it becomes a regular part of ministry in your congregation.

AVOID PRAISE YOURSELF

Finally, though it may go without saying, your efforts to solicit feedback rather than praise will be aided by setting your own example. Avoid lavishing empty praise on people in your congregation. Model the giving of feedback instead. Pastors fall into habits of praising others for many reasons. Some are legitimate and justifiable; others are not. Try not to use praise in the following ways: as a shortcut ("Super reading, as always"); as a way of avoiding conflict ("You always have good suggestions, but tonight we really need to move the meeting along"); as an attempt to protect them ("You're brilliant with kids! Next week's Sunday school class will go better"); as a means of applying subtle pressure ("You are such a lovely singer. Won't you join the choir?"); and others. If you must give praise, try to take the time to tailor it to what a person did. Remember that praising the people in your community for who they are inevitably reifies differences based on traits and qualities that they can do little to change. Speaking theologically, it does not leave as much room for the work of the Holy Spirit to create something wonderfully new in people.

A practice of feedback may at first feel alien in a ministry context, and in your role as pastor you may feel especially pressured to be the prime praise giver in the community. If you persist in modeling feedback, however, you may not only get what you need yourself but also show your congregation a whole new way of caring for one another and growing in faith together.

DANIEL KNEW SOME THINGS King Belshazzar did not. Smart is not who you are but something you work at. True power, therefore, rests not in praising or being praised for one's gifts but in faithfully and generously exercising them. Take a cue from Daniel: let other people keep their rewards for themselves; nevertheless, do what you can for the good of the kingdom.

CHAPTER

Maybe She's Born with It; Maybe It's Mentoring

IN THE INTRODUCTION TO THIS BOOK, I talked about a study undertaken by a sociologist who had immersed himself in the world of competitive swimming to figure out why some swimmers made it to the Olympics and others did not. What factors explain the excellence of top swimmers? Dan Chambliss wanted to know. The point of his study, and my use of it, is emphatically *not* to obsess about greatness or suggest that it's all about getting to the top in swimming or ministry or any other field. Instead, my points are twofold. First, *greatness* can be defined in more than one way so that no pastor is absolved from striving for it, whether one leads small membership congregations or a megachurch. Second, and most important, greatness is not as mysterious as we sometimes make it out to be. In particular, sometimes really good practitioners become really good because of the company they keep.

This chapter and the next two encourage readers who seek to become better ministers to be more intentional about keeping company with those who have something to teach. Too often we think, as the previous chapter showed, that the level of success we reach is in our genes and therefore others can't really change us. But growing and thriving in ministry happens in many ways and is due to many factors both within and beyond our control. One significant way we can contribute to our own growth as ministers is by associating with other ministers who know things we don't, who understand and approach the ministry differently than us, and whose habits and perspectives challenge or improve upon ours. In that way we help control the direction in which we progress. We stretch ourselves and become, in a very real sense, new creations.

This chapter is devoted to mentoring. Mentoring has become very popular in business and other circles; there are now many books on the subject and many formal programs developed to pair people with the right mentors. But mentoring has always informally gone on; being mentored simply means courting the company and counsel of someone who does what you do better than you currently do it. Any athlete who has played a sport—or musician, an instrument—at the same level for a long time and who suddenly gets a chance to play with a better team or group will recognize the importance of being stretched by others. It wasn't until I got to college, for instance, that I fell in with better flutists from whom I picked up better habits. Among other things, I discovered that they listened to multiple recordings of a piece to learn different ways of playing it. I don't think I had even known before then of the existence of listening studios available for that purpose, let alone considered that you would dedicate that much time and effort to your music. Those flutists simply set the bar higher than I would have set it for myself had I not entered the world of a good undergraduate music department. During my junior year, I attended an institution that also had a conservatory of music, and there I hung out with people who were in training to become professional musicians. I discovered that their habits and disciplines were even more rigorous still than those of an undergraduate music department; these students lived, breathed, and ate music in a way that I realized I never would. They not only spent more time in the practice room but they also put a whole different quality of effort into what they did.

The importance of getting out of your league and into a new world was underscored by the study on swimming. One thing Chambliss discovered was that, contrary to what one might think, *progress* did not really characterize the path of the top swimmers, at least not progress in the steady upward way we typically envision. Accumulating more and more skill by working steadily harder in the pool did not necessarily lead to swimming success; rather, changing coaches or strokes or training regimens did. Quality rather than quantity mattered. A swimmer could make a big improvement in speed by committing to one significant improvement in practice. In addition, the clearly stratified worlds of competitive swimming, it turns out, all have their own cultures, standards, attitudes, and habits. Both discipline and performance are successively redefined for a swimmer who leaves the community league for regional meets and then nationals. Chambliss found that to improve, swimmers had to break away from old patterns and adopt new ways. They left behind familiar pools, coaches, and friends, and found new ones. He wrote, "It is not by doing increasing amounts of work that one becomes excellent, but rather by changing the kinds of work."[1] And changing the people who influence you helps change the quality of work you do.

My own experience in ministry confirms this wisdom. I have been consistently stretched by keeping company with new people. Sometimes this has been hard because I feel like a fish out of water when I first connect with them, but mostly it has been immensely gratifying. When I became a divinity student I found to my delight that I was immersed in a whole community of people who thought theologically. I hadn't known you could find so many people like that in one place at one time! Their theological minds were sharp and witty and a great deal of fun. I will never forget how, during the first evening of new student orientation, one of the senior students told a denominational joke, and the others followed with one joke after another. I had never been exposed to religious humor before and realized with sudden clarity that I had entered a whole new world and wasn't in "Kansas" anymore. Chapel services at divinity school were richer than I had ever known because of students' facility with a wider range of liturgical traditions than my own. I met people who (unlike me) could actually cite Scripture passages in conversation and articulate their meaning. Later, when I was a newly ordained pastor and member of a denominational colleague group, and still later, when I worked with pastors and priests across Connecticut and with other field educators across North America as director of a supervised ministry program, I encountered practitioners whose depth of practice, pastoral skill, and theological agility continued to teach me new things. Every time I have moved into a new realm within the ministry, I have not only discovered new levels of excellence but have also been pressed to develop new attitudes and habits by those who have been at it longer than I.

Being mentored, as we shall see, is about more than just hanging around the right people. You also have to set about figuring which individuals you want to cultivate relationships with. You have to be intentional, whether you want to medal at the Olympics or make disciples. I did not realize this at first, and it took me awhile into my ministry to learn to initiate relationships. I was lucky to have people who drew me under their wings. As local church minister Brian A. Williams writes, "We cannot simply decide one morning ten or fifteen years after graduation to reinvent ourselves as the humble and wise person we always envisioned. We have to become that person."[2] But the reason I emphasize the importance even just of falling in with new people is to underscore the fact that others play a significant role in most of our achievements. We do not reinvent ourselves *by* ourselves. We need others. If we want to become, for example, wiser or more humble, we stand a far greater chance of doing so if we attach ourselves to people who embody wisdom and humility. All the more reason, then, to find the right individuals to turn to.

Resistance to Mentoring

When I would ask clergy who were training to become field education supervisors how they learned to do what they do, most of them could cite an influential figure from their early days who showed them the ropes. But not all of them would point to such a person. Some would reach instead for an individualistic explanation. They would mention some aspect of their personality ("I have always been willing to try new things") or good fortune ("The position just fell into my lap"). Either mentoring was absent from their experience or they do not give it the credit it deserved. In particular, when asking pastors to recall how they were formed as ministers early on, I have been struck by how often I hear a story of being thrown alone into the deep end of the pool to sink or swim. Take, for example, Presbyterian pastor and author Wallace M. Alston Jr.'s account of his transition from seminary to parish: "The transition from academic life, where institutions provide hospitable contexts for nurturing ideas and communities, to the isolating and often lonely life of a minister can be daunting indeed. In the past, there had been parents, teachers, senior officers, and mentors of one sort or another to provide guidance and direction. . . . Now there was no requirement, no standardized guideline, and no one to tell me what I was to do."[3] Parents, teachers, senior officers, and mentors seemed to disappear upon his stepping foot in the parish. L. Gregory Jones and Susan Pendleton

Jones, theologians and United Methodist ministers, write of eventually being mentored during their first calls but admit to finding mentors later rather than sooner and realizing that some of their colleagues never found anyone: "It took us too long in our first settings of pastoral ministry to discover the importance of mentors and to identify those from whom we could learn. Eventually we found a couple of people whose friendship and wisdom became critically important to our being sustained in ministry and in learning better practices. Yet we have also grieved as we have learned, after the fact, of gifted young pastors whose loneliness and isolation were key factors leading them to leave the pastorate and seek other vocations."[4]

The reasons ministers fail to develop relationships with mentors are probably many. It may not readily occur to those who would *serve* as mentors, for one thing, to step forward, so there may be a shortage of mentors. Many pastors connect in their minds the lessons they learned with the contexts in which they learned them. In particular, lessons learned by having survived a difficult and trying experience are forever associated with difficulty and survival. So if they learned how to pastor churches by struggling in solitude, they may tend to think, whether consciously or not, that all new pastors just have to learn that way. They may even be proud at some level of the fact that they were thrown into the pool and figured out how to swim all on their own. Without really thinking about it, they translate that pride into an expectation that their junior colleagues will do the same. This is not to say clergy share a widespread belief that "because I had to suffer, so you too should have to suffer," but rather that many experienced ministers were not mentored and therefore do not think of themselves as potential mentors, make themselves available as mentors, or invite new clergy into such a relationship.

A second reason ministers may not cultivate mentoring relationships is that many of them accept the notion that, unlike other kinds of professionals, after their schooling is over, they will learn on their own because ministry is by nature solitary. (We will examine this assumption in greater depth in the next chapter.) Alston's account has a hint of resignation, as though he simply acquiesced to entering an "isolating and often lonely life." The Joneses refer to the ubiquitous Lone Ranger metaphor that has long shaped discourses about the ministry as a profession: "Contemporary American images of pastoral ministry, especially in mainline Protestant denominations, often envision a 'lone ranger' out in a parish doing ministry."[5]

But I wonder whether a third factor operates as well, an equally powerful idea that some are just born especially gifted and do not have to work to achieve excellence. The cosmetic company Maybelline capitalizes on that notion by suggesting in their tag line that cosmetics can help some achieve the beauty others have been lucky enough to possess from birth. ("Maybe she's born with it. Maybe it's Maybelline.") Do clergy prefer to think that good ministers are born rather than made? Whenever I talk with seasoned practitioners about doing more to support and encourage excellence among novices in their field, I encounter this thinking: "But some young women and men are just naturally gifted and therefore better than others." Some go on to finish the implication: "There's little I can add to that. They either have it, or they don't." Even when I ask them to call to mind individuals they know who are exceptionally good at what they do and then ask how they got to be so good, many fall back on the idea of raw talent or genius. It's as though a person's inborn gifts—not her training or coaching or mentoring—set her apart from the rest and explain her achievement. I often hear stories of how Johnny and Janie, now at the top of their field, were amazing even as young children, their precocious talents clearly pointing to future success. I have become convinced that much of our society is enamored with the myth of inborn talent. As I write this, several popular television programs showcase the abilities of amateur singers and dancers who compete for the votes of judges and audience to become the best. These shows love to exploit the stories of amazingly talented individuals who seemingly came out of nowhere. "You don't have to come from a big city," pleaded one of the finalists on *So You Think You Can Dance* when interviewed about the path he had followed to make it to the show, the implicit argument being that *anyone* could become a great dancer if they had his moves.[6] The accompanying video chronicling his success featured many shots of him in his backyard surrounded by cornfields, as though he were simply plucked from rural America and transported to Hollywood. Less prominent in the video were shots of him working in the dance studio where he had trained under a coach for a long time. (To give the show credit, it does consistently feature footage of all the dancers in practice, working hard with professional choreographers to learn their dances.)

In the previous chapter, I detailed the connection between our love of praise and our preference for thinking that ministerial traits are given to some and fixed from birth. I examined how effort is frequently overlooked as an explanation for excellence, even sometimes belittled. In this chapter, I will take the argument a step further and say that in addition to *both* giftedness *and* effort, mentors play a significant role in developing excellence.

The Classic Mentoring Relationship

What is a mentor? The term traces its roots to Greek mythology. Mentor was the close friend of Odysseus to whom Odysseus entrusted his son Telemachus when he departed to fight the Trojan War. Mentor guided Telemachus and, as he grew, helped him become a man worthy of being his father's son. Over time the term has developed many meanings, but the basic idea is that a mentor is a wise, trusted, and experienced person who takes an interest in the life and career of a novice and commits to helping him or her grow into a role.

Though the concept comes from mythology, you need not invest the mentoring relationship with mythic significance, nor do you even have to use the term. As one writer who has served as a mentor numerous times put it, "Over the years various men and women have invited me to walk with them on a portion of their journey. Sometimes we called it mentoring; sometimes we called it lunch."[7] A mentor is, fundamentally, someone you want to hang around, someone you admire and whose wisdom you instinctively trust. In my own experience, many mentors have in fact been my peers. Mentors need not have special credentials or training, nor does mentoring have to become a science. As Brian A. Williams says, "mentoring is not about the imposition of a technique or logarithm that two participants can apply in order to produce a desired or expected result. It is much more spontaneous, unpredictable, and unrefined than that."[8] It is in some respects like friendship. But mentors *are* different in important respects from all the other friends with whom you have lunch. They have something—whether it is experience or a special perspective or a form of expertise—that you need. They are people you have a sense you could learn a lot from. A mentoring relationship, while not necessarily formal, is an intentional one. After all, it's a *relationship*, not just a chance encounter between a novice and an elder. The two of you intentionally seek each other out for regular conversations that have as their focus your growth.

Mentoring is a relationship that develops over time. You don't have one lunch with someone and get to call them your mentor, but if the two of you agree to have lunch once a month or once a year and make ministry your topic, that is closer to mentoring. A single conversation once influenced my work for years, but, again, I would not call that conversation partner a mentor. One of the reasons it's important to seek out another person for regular, sustained dialogue is that if you really care about your ministerial career, you want to commit yourself to growth in it, not just to solving the problems of the moment. Even though it may seem selfish, being mentored is about *you* and your development, not just the things you have to learn to complete the tasks at hand. Ultimately, someone agrees to mentor you because they care about who you are and where you are headed and not simply that you do a good job.

Two other features that define mentoring, even though they do not necessarily match the classic myth of Mentor and Telemachus, are, first, that mentoring be voluntary and, second, that the mentee take at least some of the initiative. Some workplaces and institutions have mandatory mentoring programs whereby new members of the community are assigned an advisor who is supposed to meet with them and help them along. These programs have merit, but a truly effective relationship is one in which the mentee wants to be mentored. As I shall emphasize throughout this book, the sure way to continue in your formation is to participate actively in creating your own opportunities for growth. As an adult learner, moreover, you will likely only learn those things you have determined you want to learn. When you identify how you want to improve and who can best help you do so, you have a better chance of succeeding.

Functionalist Mentoring

The 2009 film *Up in the Air* portrays an executive named Ryan Bingham who mentors a junior associate named Natalie Keener.[9] I use this film because their relationship sheds light on several features of a particular kind of mentoring I call *functionalist mentoring*. Theirs is not initially a voluntary relationship, but in other respects their relationship fits the pattern I have outlined. The mentor, Ryan, is a corporate downsizing expert who works for a firm solicited by companies having to lay off their employees. He travels around the country, meeting face to face with workers to break the news that they have been let go and to counsel them about their transition into new work. To many, his job and his lifestyle would be unenviable (he traveled 322 days during the previous year), but he has developed a knack for what he does and takes pride in his abilities. Natalie is a fresh-faced recent college graduate, top of her class at Cornell University, who has just been brought on by Ryan's firm to help revolutionize the layoff industry. Armed with a lot of textbook psychology and a good dose of technological savvy, she has created a system whereby the layoff conversations with workers can be conducted from remote locations, thus obviating the need for travel and saving the firm money.

Ryan objects. He immediately sees that while Natalie may know a great deal about how to navigate virtual reality she knows little about the realities of laying people off. "I'm sorry," he tells their boss, "but I don't think having a MySpace page entitles you to rewire an entire company." He persuades the boss at least to let him show Natalie the ropes by having her accompany him on several upcoming trips. Thus Natalie becomes Ryan's sidekick and, in effect, his mentee.

First, he teaches her some practical travel skills: what kind of suitcase to use and how to pack it efficiently, ways to move more swiftly through security lines, and how to accumulate the most frequent flyer miles possible using a corporate expense account. At the outset of their first trip, Ryan tests her to see whether she knows what she has gotten into. "Natalie, what is it you think we do here?" She responds with an answer straight out of the promotional literature: "We prepare the newly unemployed for the emotional and physical hurdles of job hunting while minimizing legal blowback."

"That's what we're *selling*; that's not what we're *doing*."

(Impatiently) "OK, what are we *doing*?"

"We are here to make limbo tolerable—to ferry wounded souls across the river of dread to the point where hope is dimly visible. And then you stop the boat, shove them in the water, and make them swim."

Natalie is unimpressed by Ryan's overblown metaphor. "That was really impressive," she says sarcastically. "You going to put that in your book?"

But then she watches him in action. Ryan invites her simply to observe and listen to a conversation he conducts, and when she does, she sees a different side of him and their mission. Watching him win the trust of a particularly belligerent worker using the same kinds of cliches as "ferrying across the river of dread to hope," she starts to appreciate that though their job may require some display of false compassion, there is nevertheless an art to it. Ryan actually succeeds in making the man feel hopeful about his future. Her dawning realization that there may be more to laying people off than she thought comes about because of the way he mentors her by example.

One day he decides she is ready to tackle a client conversation on her own. As they enter the corporate offices where they have been summoned, he reminds her that she must not become apologetic or emotional. She is giving workers what may potentially be the worst news of their lives, and her own feelings pale in comparison. Nevertheless, after her first conversation is over, Ryan shows genuine compassion for how she is doing. He knows this is hard work and wants her to do well. A long list of workers to be laid off remains, and he offers to take over the conversations when she starts to feel overwhelmed. At one point during her apprenticeship, their boss pushes Natalie harder than Ryan thinks she is ready for and Ryan objects to his push. Another time, Ryan defends her capability before the boss and argues that she should be given another chance. Throughout their time working together, he continually gauges her readiness for the tasks ahead by watching carefully to see whether she has taken on more than she can handle.

Though Ryan and Natalie are close, one would not characterize their relationship as particularly harmonious. In fact, it is often contentious. He is a baby boomer and she is a member of generation Y. They approach their work differently and simply care about different things. Her cavalier dismissal of his pet projects at times leaves him speechless. Nevertheless, when it comes to his commitment to her professional development,

Ryan always has her back. When news arrives that someone she had laid off committed suicide—a woman who had talked of jumping off a bridge in a way that seemed a joke at the time—Ryan insists that in no way could Natalie have foreseen the tragedy and that she could not be held liable.

In the end, Natalie quits the company after hearing of the suicide. Presumably finding it just too disheartening, she jettisons the layoff business she had worked so hard to revolutionize and disappears with little warning. Nevertheless, Ryan's final act as mentor is writing her a letter of recommendation for a job in another industry. She had previously been offered and turned down the position, so she particularly needs someone to vouch for her. He comes through with a letter simply assuring her new employer that he would not regret hiring this young woman. "I hope this guy is right about you," says the new boss, as he offers her a handshake.

Let me call mentors of the sort Ryan Bingham was for Natalie Keener *functionalist mentors*. Another kind of mentor helps mentees dig deeper into the presuppositions defining their jobs and sometimes even encourages them to challenge the status quo; I call this *transformative mentoring* and will discuss it later in this chapter. Ryan challenged Natalie and sometimes his boss, but never questioned the job; if anything, he wanted to preserve the status quo within it. Functionalist mentors, as the name implies, help mentees function effectively in their contexts. They draw upon their own expertise to show novices the ropes according to prevailing practices and patterns. In ministry contexts, functionalist mentors will likely be denominational or ecumenical colleagues who are willing to take others under their wing. I have in mind the pastor of a church in a neighboring town, a colleague at another institution, or a fellow member of the guild or professional association. (I am assuming that most clergy don't have a senior person working alongside them in the same workplace day to day as Natalie did.) Bishops and other ecclesial superiors may also make good mentors of this sort, for it is often their role to induct others and provide them oversight and guidance.

SKILL DEVELOPMENT

Functionalist mentors, first of all, help you develop the skills that will round out the competence you bring to your ministry. Mentors are generally to be distinguished from teachers or trainers, so you don't usually turn to them to help you learn brand new things, but they can help you sort out your options, steer you away from unwise moves, reflect with you on how your projects seem to be going, and so forth. Unless they happen to work alongside you, they may not be able to offer firsthand observations on how you are doing. Incidentally, mentoring differs in this way from the process of giving feedback I discussed in the previous chapter. But mentors can give advice and counsel upon hearing you describe your work.

For example, about a year into my first pastoral position in a church, I was asked to perform a wedding. This was something I had not done before. Not for real, that is. In the course on liturgy I had taken in divinity school, I had designed and conducted a mock wedding (for which I persuaded two of my friends to play the parts of bride and groom). This learning experience meant that I was not completely lacking in competence: I had developed a theological outlook on the meaning of wedding ceremonies, I had learned their central liturgical components, and I possessed a basic notion of what to do when. But as a novice, I had never prepared an actual couple for the liturgy, nor had I time to learn much about methods of premarital counseling. To top it off, I myself had never been married and was uniting two people who had both been married before. I was, in many ways, like the character Natalie who had a lot of book smarts but little actual experience. Needless to say, I was nervous. I confessed all this to a colleague, and she graciously invited me to her office to see how she handled weddings. She showed me the questionnaire she used with couples and told me how she administered it. She suggested that I meet three times with the couple for counseling and described what we could do at each meeting. As I recall, she also shared with me the terms she set for couples regarding wedding ceremonies and the elements that were nonnegotiable for her. She probably showed me some sample services. With her straightforward advice giving, she filled in my repertoire of skills and gave me exactly what I needed to be more confident and competent.

Parenthetically, I am aware that some folks would argue I should have learned all this in seminary. They criticize theological schools for inadequately preparing their graduates to function as parish pastors. But I would defend the adequacy of my preparation to that point. I had taken an excellent course from a respected pastor-theologian who instilled in me all the right theological instincts about the church's role in marriage today, lent me a few practical skills, and increased my capacity to exercise the authority I would need when I became a pastor. I just hadn't had enough time in three years to be prepared to actually marry two people. Few students have enough time during three years of seminary to learn everything and to mature in all the necessary ways to be effective pastors. Theological degrees alone cannot confer all the skills one needs. And why should they? What is wrong, after all, with learning at a colleague's feet? This is a perfectly good way to obtain the real-world education and formation that all professionals inevitably need to complement their studies. After all, in the days before academic institutions became the standard venue for clergy training they are today, apprenticeships constituted the primary way clergy learned their craft. As Williams points out, "That most preparation for pastoral ministry takes place exclusively in the seminary or university instead of in partnership with a church or a more experienced pastor is more an accident of history than a result of careful theological deliberation."[10]

In any event, my first wedding was an example of how someone took a novice aside and said, "Look, this is how I do it. You
might adapt what I do for yourself." When one has more years
of experience and confidence, mentoring for skill development
can take a different form. Your mentor can help you build on an
already solid practice by suggesting ways you might improve or
new directions you might take. For me, once I had been a field
educator for a while and the basic functions became second nature, I wanted to exercise leadership by growing the program
beyond what our school was used to. I sought out colleagues at
other schools whose programs I admired. One person in particular became a mentor to me. We served together on a board,
so I saw him twice a year. We got in the habit of going out for a
meal after the board meetings, and I would bring a mental list
of ideas I wanted to float by him and counsel I wanted to seek.
He was always interested in my questions and took them seriously, providing very thoughtful answers. I trusted his instincts
about what I should do and what I should probably avoid. I
often credited him back home when suggesting a new plan or
policy. To this day I count him as a mentor of mine.

By referring to functions and skills, I do not mean to suggest that mentors only teach you what to *do*; they also teach
you how to *be*. At some points in your development, identity
formation is really what you need most. Cleophus J. LaRue,
now a seminary professor and Baptist minister, recalls how his
pastor nurtured him and the other teenagers in their Baptist
church growing up: "He guided us not simply in the knowledge of the various functions of Christian ministry but in all
of life. He instructed us on how to dress as well as how to conduct ourselves in the church and in the community. He insisted
on a high standard of pulpit decorum and ministerial ethics.
Rev. Dilworth was modest in his manner and frowned on any
young minister who he thought had gotten 'a little too big for
his britches.'"[11] Perhaps because they had not had the benefit
of similarly forthright direction early on, several of my divinity

school students asked their supervisors to coach them on what they termed *presence:* how they came across at coffee hour, during meetings, and in informal interactions with parishioners. In my own experience of being new to a position of responsibility, I can recall one particularly exasperating day at work when my righteous temper must have gotten the better of me. My supervisor and I talked about how I could better manage the anger my job would inevitably sometimes provoke. On a lighter but equally important note, mentors can also help you immensely by offering a sense of humor. They often bring a balanced perspective to concerns you yourself are taking too seriously.

ENCULTURATION

A second gift mentors give, besides identity and skill development, is that of enculturation. They help you fit in and get along. In effect, they socialize you into the way things are done in your "shop." Although this may sound mundane, it is no small thing. We all need someone to guide us when we don't yet know the parameters of appropriateness—behaviors that are standard practice versus those that might raise eyebrows. Every ministry setting has its own culture, and we succeed when we learn to operate within it. Walter Wright, who has written extensively on mentoring, especially in the business world, describes how he drew upon a mentor when he took a new position. As a United States citizen assuming the presidency of Regent College in British Columbia, Wright realized that he didn't know enough about Canada. Looking back, he admits how naive he was: "Like many in the United States, I thought of Canada as a familiar extension to the North—more like another state than a different culture. Wrong! Canadians may speak the same language but they have their own history, traditions, and culture with subtle differences that can trip up a new president. If I was going to travel across this country, recruiting students, raising money, and representing the school, I had a steep learning curve about things Canadian."[12] Wright identified a colleague to become his mentor in this area. "Doug taught me what I needed to know, raised questions to help me understand what I was learning, corrected my cultural faux pas, and pointed me toward resources to enrich my perspective."[13]

Wright's is a literal example of needing to understand the culture of a new setting. Mentors can help you unpack the more subtle aspects of culture as well. In parish ministry, for example, congregations differ greatly depending on size, class, ethnicity, denomination, geographical location, and other cultural features.

CAREER COUNSELING

Finally, having a functionalist mentor can also be particularly useful when you want to know how to move ahead with your career. If you are an academic in a certain sort of institution, for example, you can unwittingly throw yourself into educational and administrative activities that will do little, regrettably, to help you get tenure. But if no one points out the unwritten rules, you won't realize why you get overlooked for promotion when your review rolls around. In the church, colleagues can share from their experience the things search committees most care about and the ways you might develop yourself in order to seek a position of greater responsibility, if that is your goal. In the past this kind of mentoring was sometimes called *grooming*. The term is reminiscent of an era whereby following the right rules more predictably led to success: if you were groomed to become the boss's successor, you would most likely get the job. Those days are gone (thankfully, for many of us, as they were also the days of exclusionary old boys' networks), but there is still something to the idea that a trusted senior colleague can help you discern the ways to become more rather than less successful on your chosen path.

Functionalist mentors have their place in ministry. I hasten to point out that mentoring relationships do not benefit younger clergy only. Your need to be mentored does not end as you age; indeed, you should seek out mentors whenever you assume new roles. Having mentors to talk to may in fact become especially important as you become more seasoned, because the people who report to you may become less frank. While people in your congregation or organization no doubt possess a great deal of wisdom, they might be less inclined to share it with you if they perceive you as a leader or authority figure. As we can infer from the discussion in the previous chapter, they might be inclined simply to offer praise. Wright wisely acknowledges, "People do not readily argue with the leader,"[14] and congregants might think anything they offer short of praise will sound like argument. But you will continue to need advice and counsel throughout your career. No less an experienced voice than United Methodist Bishop and theologian William Willimon has argued for the necessity of mentoring upon entering a new context: "My wife, Patsy, and I have noticed that since coming to this new ministry in Alabama, we feel oddly younger—as if we're in the first days of our marriage, as if we're at our very first church. I think it may be because the church has called me to a ministry for which I have no experience, few qualifications, and little knowledge. I have to ask for help, read boring business books on management, *and get a coach*—like I was twenty-something. And it's wonderful to be young!"[15] Willimon does acknowledge that being mentored may not come as easily for seasoned pastors: "It's easy to ask questions, seek help, crave mentoring, and learn new skills when you are just starting out—when you are unsteady, green, and goofy. But that's hard for those of us over fifty. We have been in this ministry so long we think we actually know just how to do ministry."[16] Nevertheless, he recognizes the importance and even the necessity for pastors like himself to cultivate humility, admit what they don't know, and identify the things they could still stand to learn. He even makes it a theological imperative: "We cannot worship a living God without continually turning and becoming like a little child."[17]

Transformative Mentoring

Functionalist mentoring is not all that clergy need, however. If we want to honor a living God, as Willimon challenges us to do, we have to stay alive to the ever-changing realities transforming the church into a place to work different from what it was even a decade ago. Like other "industries," ours is in the process of rapid change, and we all must find ways to adapt with creativity and integrity. One way is to intentionally cultivate relationships with people who not only have expertise to share but who also can challenge the status quo. Only someone who has the ability to *transform* and not just *conform to* the prevailing customs and practices in ministry will help us weather the evolving changes.

To complement functionalist mentoring, then, you also need what might be called *transformative mentoring*. What are the differences? Functionalist mentoring aims, as the previous examples have shown, at improvement and reinforcement. Your mentor helps you work at your skills so that you can better perform within the system and do well. She exposes you to new ideas, models excellent behavior for you, perhaps even shields you from failure. (The word *protégé* is derived from the same root as *protection*.) Mentors describe options to you that have worked well in the past for them. Their tips and suggestions are based on their current understanding of the context in which you both labor. The methods of functionalist mentoring are advice driven and didactic. Functionalist mentoring does not necessarily have as its aim altering the underlying system. Functionalist mentors primarily help you fit in, get along, and advance. They do not necessarily question the assumptions that have shaped the profession or the institution but rather take them for granted. Having a functionalist mentor is like having a sponsor who shoulders some responsibility for helping you succeed within the enterprise, as the enterprise has been defined. As such, functionalist mentoring tends to replicate and reinforce existing power relations and may reproduce existing biases and even injustices.

Transformative mentoring, in contrast, aims at change. Your mentor does not just inspire and motivate you but also tests you. Prevailing reality also gets tested. The focus of your conversations with a transformative mentor is not only on how to do things better but also on what things are necessary to do in the first place. Few assumptions are taken for granted. Even the underlying aims of your vocation and your institutional context are taken apart and examined. Together you do not just examine options that have been proven to work but also wonder about options that lie "outside the box." Having a transformative mentor is like having a dialogue partner who challenges you to look beyond the ways your current on-the-job reality has been constructed to ways it might be de- and reconstructed. This kind of mentoring thus demands mutual reflection. Its methods are more Socratic than didactic, centered more on questions than advice.

Since I drew from popular culture for an image of functionalist mentoring, I will do the same for transformative mentoring. The television show *Numb3rs*, which aired on the CBS network from 2005 to 2010, features two mathematicians, Charlie Eppes and Larry Fleinhardt.[18] Charlie is the brother of an FBI agent, and he moonlights as a consultant to the bureau, helping them solve crimes by applying mathematical theories and equations. Larry is Charlie's mentor, an often eccentric genius whose intellectual interests range from math to new age spirituality. In the opening episode of the series, Charlie is frustrated because the equation he had designed to narrow the location of a murder suspect within Los Angeles has failed to produce anyone. He is so upset that he can't concentrate on a new attempt, so he bicycles through the rain over to the video game arcade where Larry is absorbed in playing.

"Larry, something went wrong and I don't know what, and now I can't even think."

"Well, let me guess. You tried to solve a problem in human behavior and it blew up in your face."

"Yeah, pretty much."

"OK, well, Charles, you are a mathematician. You are always looking for the elegant solution. Human behavior is rarely if ever elegant." (He says this while both of them watch his string of winning scores displayed on the video screen.) "The universe is full of these odd bumps and twists. You know, perhaps you need to make your equation less elegant, more complicated, less precise, more descriptive. It's not going to be as pretty but it might work a little bit better." (They ponder the idea in silence for a moment.) "Charlie, when you're working on human problems, there's going to be pain and disappointment. You've got to ask yourself: Is it worth it?"

The next scene shows Charlie flipping through FBI file photos of all the victims from the case. Then he goes back to his whiteboard, presumably having decided that the pain and disappointment are indeed worth it. In the end, he combines two equations into a more complicated one that yields the information the FBI needs to find their suspect. Just as Larry had predicted, the final means to the solution wasn't as pretty, but it did work better.

SKILL DEVELOPMENT

Transformative mentors can help you with some of the same things as functionalist mentors—skill development, understanding prevailing culture, and career counseling—but they redefine each. Many years ago when I was still new to my role as associate pastor, I needed to develop skills in youth ministry. The youth group program had gone dormant and I had been asked to begin working to resurrect it, despite the fact that the church included very few families with youth anymore. I met with the pastor and others in the congregation who were mentoring me to discuss the challenge. They suggested steps I could take: First, call on all the families and get to know them and the youth. Then, I should set a first meeting date and plan an engaging set of activities. We brainstormed some more ideas together. I was still somewhat dubious, but those who were advising me countered that too many of the adults in church had been asking why there was no youth group in the church, especially now that I was on board. Apparently growing a youth program was, to some, an expectation of my hire.

In the course of these conversations about youth ministry in the church, I traveled back to divinity school for a visit and sat down for coffee with one of my former advisors (I'll call her Connie). I talked with her about the challenges being put to me. I explained that the church used to have a flourishing youth program that I was expected to revive, though I was dubious about the prospects for a traditional youth group there. Connie asked me what kinds of things adults in the church were saying to see whether I could name their memories and hopes for youth ministry. Together we identified a subtle discourse operating among some at the church: "We're afraid this church might stop growing, and the youth represent future growth. A youth group is a sign of hope for our church." Connie then asked me what participation in my own youth group had meant to me, and after hearing that it had conferred on me a sense of respect as a leader in the church, Connie pointed out that another discourse about youth ministry was possible: "The youth represent our present, and we should minister with and to them in all the same ways we do adults." According to this discourse, a youth group becomes but one way to carry out a ministry with youth. Connie then brainstormed some alternatives with me. I returned to work at the church and presented a different plan: in addition to calling on all the families, I would build relationships with each youth member, pair them with a mentor, include them in the fellowship and retreat ministries of the church currently targeting only adults, and find a way for each youth member to serve on a committee or ministry alongside adults.

The folks in the church were serving as good functionalist mentors for me. They were helping me develop some of the skills necessary to youth ministry: recruitment, planning, and leading activities. Connie, however, was my transformative mentor. She showed me that being a youth minister required even more and different skills, including those of persuasion, inclusion, empowerment, and relationship building. In addition, she gently led me away from considering only immediate next steps toward considering what would be the best form of youth ministry for our church in the long run. She redefined skilled youth ministry for me. She also helped me unpack the prevailing discourse at the church, knowing that I would have to take people's attitudes into account no matter what youth programming I undertook. She knew that unless I understood what shaped the thinking of the members of my church, I might misinterpret any resistance to my plan.

It should be acknowledged, of course, that part of the reason Connie was able to mentor me the way that she did was that she did not work at my church. She was an outsider to my setting. Therefore, it was not so much her direct expertise that she brought to my dilemma about youth ministry as it was her ability to reflect upon my dilemma based on her years of experience. Often it is easier for someone outside a system to suggest the transformative but difficult steps that should be taken within it. (Some transformative mentors even come from outside the clergy's vocation when they are located, say, primarily in the academy rather than the local church.) Outsiders are neither answerable to nor responsible for the community whose changes they are recommending, so they are often freer to imagine new possibilities and bolder at naming the forms of resistance those possibilities trigger.

ENCULTURATION

Transformative mentors also engage in enculturation, but instead of simply helping you fit in by coaching you the way Wright was coached in ways Canadian, they can also help you examine cultural assumptions. When I was about two years into being a field educator, I traveled to the biennial conference of our guild and was eating lunch in a restaurant near the conference hotel where I happened to end up talking to a colleague from a peer institution whom I had not yet met. As is sometimes the case at professional meetings, that time at lunch ended up being some of the best-spent time the entire weekend. In fact, I used her insights for years to come. What she did was help me see how the roles and responsibilities of field educators had been constructed over the years according to certain assumptions about the place of field education within theological education. (That is, field education was often still marginalized because internships were considered jobs seminarians did on the side of their *real* education and not *bona fide* courses in the curriculum. In such a culture, field educators were considered student service administrators, not teachers.) But she also told me how the culture was changing and that many field educators were now successfully claiming a new role. I returned home and started working little by little to make changes that would bring my work in line with the perspective she had opened up for me. If I had been smarter, I would have tried to turn that chance encounter into an ongoing mentoring relationship, as I probably would have benefitted from continued dialogue with someone who had made such a difference to my work in one conversation.

Frequently transformative mentors help you examine your culture by asking incisive questions of you. Ryan's question of Natalie—"What is it you think we do here?"—may have been lobbed as a challenging retort, but it was actually a pretty sophisticated question posed to a beginner, especially one who was failing to see the forest for the trees. Ryan helped Natalie see that what they were doing was promoting a culture of hope rather than despair, even as they were laying people off from their jobs. That most famous asker of questions, Socrates, always forced his mentees to see reality in new ways. He was the master of asking the "powerful question," what field educator Susan Fox argues is "the essential coaching tool for prompting deep learning." She describes powerful questions as ones that are "expansive" and that "evoke clarity, action, discovery, insight, or commitment; open channels of creativity; challenge existing paradigms; and stop people in their tracks."[19]

CAREER COUNSELING

Finally, to help you advance your career, transformative mentors might not simply groom you for your next job but also counsel you to consider new directions you would never have imagined on your own. Or, they might test your will for moving in a new direction. A mentor of mine once helped me see that a position I regarded as an advance in my career might just make me miserable if I were to apply for the job and get it. Another once persuaded me to stay awhile longer in a job and helped me transform it. Just as sometimes an athlete or a musician needs her coach's or teacher's help imagining the next level of performance she might move into (or not), so too ministers often need someone to expand and examine their horizons.

I hasten to say that transformative mentoring is not necessarily better than functionalist mentoring. You will find both to be important to your formation as a minister, especially at different points in your career. You will likely discover that different people you know will be better at one mentoring role than another. But I would like to make the case for transformative mentors, not only functionalist ones. This is a crucial time for the ministry vocation as we all struggle to read the tea leaves and plan for the church of the future. Individuals who may seem like good mentors because they have developed a great deal of expertise have sometimes gotten where they are by playing the game well, not necessarily by challenging its rules. One set of researchers argues that sometimes mentors can do more harm than good if they are part of a problem of stagnation in their field: "If a field is not keeping abreast with social and technical changes, then mentors can end up inducting protégés into a system of meaning and practices that no longer has the same merit, influence, or application."[20] While sometimes those on the frontier of new ministry paradigms have neither the time nor the temperament to offer others mentoring, it is worth seeking out such people. In addition, sometimes mentors represent an ethos within their field that needs changing. Certain maladies have afflicted the ministry for years, such as loneliness and the pressure to be perfect that I will discuss in the next chapter. Today's generation of pastors does not need to be mentored into an ethos that just perpetuates these problems.

I have highlighted the differences between functionalist and transformative mentoring and encouraged you to cultivate both. I have also argued that mentoring will happen at your own initiative. Mentoring will not just come along automatically, for reasons discussed at the outset. You will benefit more when your heart and mind are in it. I conclude, therefore, with some suggestions, first, on what to consider when looking for a mentor and, second, how to be a good mentee.

What to Avoid in a Mentor

Because you will look for different positive qualities in a mentor depending on what you need from the relationship, it is easier to list qualities that mentees should avoid. Roman Catholic field educator Regina Coll points out in her classic book on supervision, "We can learn a great deal by way of negatives." She even makes a theological case for identifying what a mentor is not: "In theology we speak of *via negativa* as one way of discovering what God is like. God is not . . . , God is not . . . , God is not . . . , finally leads us to surmise what God may be."[21] In that spirit, I will identify several things your mentor should *not* be.

CONTROLLING

Based on the experiences of many novices who have been (unhappily) mentored, probably the most common kind of mentor to avoid is someone who wants to control you. I hasten to say that many attempts at control can be well intentioned. Those who care that you succeed can become overly anxious about how you are doing. (Unfortunately, they often express their anxiety as control and can hover over you like helicopters, ready at any moment to correct, advise, or otherwise save you. They can stifle your freedom to the point where you become indifferent to your own improvement.) However, some attempts at control stem from less honorable intentions. Examples include withholding opportunity, defending turf, or resenting a mentee's success. One set of researchers labeled these behaviors "non-mentoring" or "anti-mentoring."[22]

Another expression of control is a desire to replicate oneself and extend one's own legacy. Sometimes it can be very hard for seasoned pastors to see that there are perfectly good ways of doing ministry that differ radically from their own. They have a deep desire to pass on what they have learned, because it worked for them and they value it. But as I used to tell internship supervisors, mentoring is not cloning. Or, as Coll says, the "first commandment of supervision" is that "You shall not try to make the seminarians into your own image and likeness; one is enough."[23] Therefore, if you sense in a potential mentor a tendency to talk excessively about himself and a rigidity with respect to how things ought to be done, you might not have found the best person.

SELF-UNAWARE

If one point of mentoring is to help you cultivate your own sense of self and ability, then you don't want to choose someone who is unaware of and inarticulate about her own gifts. She won't be able to name yours. I have often said that when seeking a good mentor, you want to discover someone who is both good at what they do and knows *why* they are good. Some people are very skilled. They might have a marvelous way of presiding in worship or be sought out by everyone for spiritual care or know how to lead others through conflict—but cannot for the life of them explain how they do these things. They just can't put their skillfulness into words. Of course, it's not always easy to articulate tacit knowledge, as we shall see in the next chapter, but unless you just want to copy what your mentor does, you will want to look for someone who can reflect on what they are doing as they are doing it. Some potential mentors, on the other hand, are quite able to reflect with you at length on theories of ministry. They love to ponder over, say, the best forms of worship leadership or spirituality or conflict management, but when observed are really not very good at these things. They cannot put what they know into practice. After all, there is *something* to the old adage that "those who can't do, teach." Ideally, what you want is someone who can demonstrate *both* tacit *and* explicit knowledge. Their practice itself should be a model and an inspiration, and they should be able to talk about the meaning of it so that you can learn from them.

In addition, you want someone who is cognizant of their own foibles and who is willing to be vulnerable before you. You don't necessarily want to imitate perfection but rather observe a realistic model of ministry. When someone can tell you about the mistakes they made, you see that ministry is not easy but mistakes can be overcome. You also discover that you don't have to be perfect. There is a limit, however, to vulnerability. You don't want someone who shares his uncertainties about ministry in a way that only adds to your own confusion.[24]

UNCURIOUS

I remember once meeting a ministerial colleague for the first time. I was hoping she would collaborate with me on a project, so I wanted to get to know her better and form a relationship that I hoped would turn into a working one. I went to her place of work where I spent about an hour receiving a tour and learning about her background, her particular interests, and her hopes and dreams for the future. I came away confident that she had a lot to contribute to the project, so that was good. However, as I was pulling out of the parking lot, I realized that she had not asked me a single question during our hour together. It was quite striking, in retrospect, how uncurious *she* had seemed about *me*. In the end I trusted that her lack of curiosity was idiosyncratic, for whatever reason, to our meeting that day, but it did make me wonder whether she would relate to others on the project the same way. Over time we formed a positive and even warm collegial relationship, changing my perception of her. I don't think I would have ever chosen her as a mentor, however, if that first meeting were all I had to go on.

A stereotypical image of being mentored may be one of perfecting your craft while quietly absorbing the wisdom of your teacher. But in reality a better image is of a mentor listening to you. Beware of colleagues who don't ask you any questions, and be on the lookout for those who do, especially if the questions are really good ones that you continue to mull over the rest of the day.

UNINSPIRED

Coll tells a joke about seasoned practitioners who have failed to continue learning: "I was once with a group of professors who were discussing the contributions of some long-term veterans of our profession when someone said that a colleague had taught forty years at the same institution. Another replied, 'No, he taught one year forty times.'"[25] Two versions of the joke I have heard are of the preacher who has not had a new thought in forty years or the theologian whose most recent illustrations about the church date back to the seventies. These are not the kind of people you want as mentors. Ask what potential mentors are reading, writing, and thinking about these days. You want someone who keeps abreast of ideas and expresses interest in new ones. Do not assume this means you must find someone young. One of my mentors continued to put me to shame well into his retirement years by asking if I had had a chance yet to read some recent publication or another. He had, and was clearly eager to discuss it with somebody. Toward the end of his life, when a book I had written came out, I sent him a copy, and in a thank-you note his wife told me that, though he was no longer able to read due to his illness, he enjoyed hearing parts of it read to him. That kind of person is a blessing upon your life.

OVERLY BUSY

Some people always have time to talk when you give them a call. Others you hesitate to "bother." Follow your instincts in this regard. A good mentor should be able to make time for you. Sometimes a person's inability to make time is no reflection on you. Mentoring requires investing time and energy, and it behooves both of you to realize this and acknowledge when time and energy are lacking.

PRAISE JUNKIE

While you want your mentor to be in your corner, you do not necessarily want someone heaping praise on you. In the previous chapter, I suggested several reasons why some ministers are addicted to praise giving. Look for someone who is good at offering feedback instead.

It is worth noting that the qualities of good mentoring do not necessarily correlate with age or position or gender. Do not limit your thinking about the kind of person who might make a good mentor.

How to Be a Good Mentee

Several years ago, seminary professors and researchers David T. Gortner and John Dreibelbis conducted an in-depth study of mentoring among priests in the Episcopal church that yielded some interesting results. Perhaps most striking was simply their finding that priests named a relationship with a mentor as the single most important influence on their development in ministry, named more often even than seminary.[26] Gortner and Dreibelbis argue, "This alone suggests the need for denominational leaders to focus more attention on mentor relationships and post-ordination training."[27] But their study did not stop there. In addition to interviewing priests about how important they perceived mentoring to be, they looked closely at how different priests *used* their mentors. For example, they asked what skills and norms priests learned from their mentors, what qualities mentees sought in mentors, and what qualities mentoring brought out in them.[28] It turns out that different sorts of mentees looked to mentors for help in improving in different aspects of ministry practice. Those who described themselves as introverted, cautious, and more ecclesiastically conformist reported being primarily interested in learning the tried-and-true skills of worship leadership and pastoral care. Interestingly enough, these priests also saw their congregations as more resistant to change and reported little church growth. Others (the minority) who were extroverted, innovative, and less conformist sought to learn the less traditional skills of communication strategies, conflict management, and networking.

Gortner and Dreibelbis also correlated their findings on mentoring with separate assessments about the effectiveness of the priests in the study. It turns out that those priests who were effective in ministry viewed their mentors as people to whom they could turn to for guidance in decision making, empowerment, and new perspectives. When given a choice between describing their mentor as "a parent," "a supervisor," "a colleague," or "a friend," effective priests split their choices roughly evenly among all four. Priests who were struggling in their ministries, by contrast, overwhelmingly compared their mentors to parents.[29] Struggling priests, in fact, tended to name as their mentors those paternal figures from their preseminary, preordination days—people who had supported their initial call to ministry—and did not talk very much about individuals who helped them continue to develop themselves and refine their skills.

These findings suggest that while it is vital to have people who will be advocates for you, encourage you, and comfort you, especially early on, it is equally if not more important to have people who will push you, think with you, and work with you to develop new skills. Priests with good mentors turned out to be priests who could assume leadership gracefully, turn to a variety of colleagues for counsel and advice, and take care of themselves. Priests without good mentors too often developed "idiosyncratic and untested approaches to leadership"[30] and were less self-confident and decisive. Mentoring ultimately increases self-reliance and decreases dependency, thus helping you move along and not remain immature and needy as a minister. It may even help your congregation grow. But you need to be open to a relationship that is challenging and not simply comforting.

To become a good mentee you will additionally want to be transparent and vulnerable with your mentor. Try not to worry about how you come across, for your mentor needs to see the real you. Try also not to resist hearing the sensitive things your mentor might be trying to say to you. You will not learn if you assume a defensive posture with your mentor. On the other hand, don't think that you have to follow slavishly everything she says, as a mentor is not your boss. Williams writes about the twin dangers of being overly hesitant or overly demonstrative: "Instead of entering openly into a mentoring friendship, we usually protect our self-created images in one of two ways, both of which are derivative of the demand for self-determination—either we fashion a hesitant self that can do no right, that can hear nothing but criticism, that eagerly molds itself to any word of counsel; or we fashion a demonstrative self that can do no wrong, hear no criticism, or heed any word of counsel."[31]

If you let them, your mentors will have a profound influence on the minister you become. The kind of minister you become is never set in stone and cannot be predicted at the outset of your career. You are not born with it. You will not be the same years into your ministry as you were at the beginning. You *will* grow and develop, one way or the other. Why not improve your chances of becoming the minister you can be proud of?

3

Heads above Water:
Peer Group Learning

As you read the previous chapter, certain individuals probably came to mind who have served as mentors for you. These individuals may have included seasoned pastors and senior colleagues, but you may have also thought of people who are your peers. Peer mentoring is very common, as we often learn as much from our own cohorts as we do from our seniors. This chapter and the following one focus on the learning we do with our peers in groups formed for the purpose of continuing education and formation. I will argue that peer groups provide an invaluable setting for thinking through the challenges of ministry and celebrating its joys. Clergy peers can help us make sense of what is happening to us. In addition to providing a welcome source of fellowship and support, they can become an intellectual community that sustains us in thinking through the challenges to our vocation and striving for excellence within it. Peer groups are not only for solving problems, then, but also for several other aspects of ministerial formation.

Ordained ministry is unique, but sometimes in descriptions of other vocations we hear echoes of what ministers say about the nature of their work. Two of my vocations besides ministry are teaching and writing, and so perhaps it is natural that I hear certain similarities among what teachers say about teaching, what writers say about writing, and what ministers say about ministry. A couple of things expressed by all three types of practitioners are, first, how lonely their work can feel and, second, how difficult it is. Hear the way Lee Shulman, president of the Carnegie Foundation for the Advancement of Teaching, recalls his early eagerness to join the professoriate, only to have discovered over the years that loneliness characterizes his profession in ways he could never have anticipated. See whether you agree that he could be describing a new pastor or priest joining the pastorate or priesthood:

> At the end of the June commencement at which I received my graduate degree, George Beadle, then president of the University of Chicago, turned to those of us baking in our robes in Rockefeller Chapel and proclaimed, "Welcome to the community of scholars." Perspiring though I was, a chill went through me because this was something I had aspired to—membership in a community of scholars.
>
> As the years have gone by, I have come to appreciate how naive was my anticipation of what it would mean to be a member of a scholarly community. My anticipation contained two visions. One was the vision of the solitary individual laboring quietly, perhaps even obscurely, somewhere in the library stacks, or in a laboratory, or at an archaeological site; someone who pursued his or her scholarship in splendid solitude. My second vision was of this solitary scholar entering the social order—becoming a member of the community—interacting with others, in the classroom and elsewhere, as a teacher.
>
> What I didn't understand as a new Ph.D. was that I had it backwards! We experience isolation not in the stacks but in the classroom. We close the classroom door and experience

pedagogical isolation, whereas in our life as scholars, we are members of active communities.[1]

Ministers, teachers, and writers also share an awareness (occasionally bordering on preoccupation) of how hard it is to do what they do. The following excerpt is taken from a humorous essay by novelist Michael Cunningham. The title of his essay, "A Writer Should Always Feel Like He's in Over His Head," affirms the love-hate relationship writers have with the challenges of writing, suggesting that while they complain about how hard their craft is, they do not truly wish it were easy. "As a novelist, I learned long ago that my interest in talking about how very difficult it is to write fiction exceeds almost everybody's interest in hearing about it." Cunningham goes on to say that all the writers he knows share his obsession and that "often when we are alone together we do, in fact, with a sense of guilty abandon, spend a certain amount of time buzzing about how unbelievably, monumentally difficult writing actually is; what fools we are for having taken it up in the first place; and how often we contemplate abandoning the pursuit altogether."[2]

If you are a seasoned minister reading this book, and even if you are a new one, you can likely identify with both the loneliness and the difficulty of doing ministry. Happily, I believe times are changing. In significant and growing numbers, clergy across denominations are discovering the practice of regularly gathering in peer groups for support and continuing education, and by doing so are discovering that belonging to a peer group undercuts their sense of loneliness. Evidence also suggests that it brings more meaning to their work, making it more satisfying if not necessarily easier. In fact, I am convinced that the practice of peer groups is contributing to the emergence of a new kind of minister and to a new kind of ministerial formation. The changes cannot come soon enough. The reality is that ministry *can be* quite a lonely and difficult vocation; there is no doubt about that. I need not repeat here the statistics about clergy burnout and dropout; suffice it to say that ministers not only *contemplate* abandoning the pursuit of ministry (as Cunningham says of writers), but they also *do* regularly leave ministry—especially congregational ministry—for other lines of work. While peer groups may not entirely reverse the migration away from the profession, they can help us clergy reframe, reconstruct, and revitalize our work and our perspectives on our work. This, in turn, has the ripple effect of revitalizing the ministries in which we are engaged, which benefits everyone.

Three Realities

While there may be something to the idea that as ministers we should always feel like we are "in over our head" (or else we may not be taking our calling seriously enough), I gave this chapter the title I did because, while ministry may demand our utmost, there is no point in drowning! Joining with our peers to figure out what makes ministry so hard can help us keep our heads above water. Traditionally, professional ministry has been considered hard in at least three ways: it can be lonely, monumentally difficult, and prone to inauthenticity. However, we see signs today that pastors are changing all three realities. Indeed, there are many members of the clergy who are *not* struggling and who want to join peer groups because they relish the chance to reflect on work they enjoy (even if they find it challenging) and desire to improve. Peer groups are, in short, for those who are keeping their heads above water and want to stay there.

OVERCOMING LONELINESS IN MINISTRY

Pastors need to get a collective grasp, first of all, on what contributes to the loneliness they experience. I am not pointing out anything new by saying that the ministry is considered a lonely pursuit. Nearly every conference I attend or piece I read on the formation of ministers stresses our need somehow to change the culture of loneliness for clergy and other religious leaders. At some point, someone invariably brings up the metaphor of the Lone Ranger, implying that ministry may be compared to traveling all alone across a vast landscape. Indeed, loneliness in their work is frequently given as a primary reason why ministers seek out their colleagues. Many acknowledge that ministers are hungry for the companionship of others. I am reminded of a scene Richard Lischer describes in his memoir of his first years in ministry in rural southern Illinois. He would gather monthly with the other Lutheran pastors in the area. They would have Bible study, share refreshments, and then celebrate the Eucharist. Some of the older pastors in the group subscribed to the belief that the Eucharist should only be received from a member of the clergy, and therefore those monthly gatherings became for them the only time they took communion. Lischer's story gives new meaning to being hungry for the community of one's peers![3] Simply belonging to a group of peers that gathers regularly, whether it be for fellowship, spiritual formation, or continuing education, can go a long way toward meeting clergy's felt need to break out of their isolation.

And yet the experience of isolation, as hard as it can be, does not by itself explain the loneliness of ministry. Ministers do not simply experience a lack of company. The Lone Ranger metaphor is not really apt, for ministers do not really spend all that much time *alone*. (Indeed they often complain about just the opposite: the clamoring of other people after their attention; the endless rounds of meetings, appointments, and events crowding their calendar; and the constant ring of the phone and ping of the e-mail server.) No, if anything ministers tend instead to report that they long for more solitary, quiet moments in their days. They do not necessarily desire the presence of more people. Therefore I don't think peer groups are simply meeting a need for companionship. As Lischer's story points out, they meet a need for the companionship of peers *who do the same thing they do*. The nature of their work often keeps them from rubbing shoulders with peers in the everyday

exercise of their calling, something many other kinds of professionals more readily enjoy. Having a peer group provides them
at least some time in their ministry where they can be among
those who occupy the same role as they do and who share similar, if not the same, experiences. Ministers yearn for the company of others who get what they are going through.

This brings us back to Shulman's description of the loneliness academics experience and the importance to all who care
about good practice of attending to the real cause of their isolation. As a newly minted academic, Shulman thought that it
would be the hours spent in solitude pursuing his scholarship
that would be lonely. Instead, he found that isolation occurs
when the teacher enters the classroom and closes the door.
Why should this be? Wouldn't a classroom full of learners be
less lonely than the quiet of the library or lab? From the perspective of satisfying one's needs for extroversion, perhaps. But
faced with a classroom of students, the teacher *is* isolated in
the following sense: she is the only one in the room who occu-
pies *her* role. There are rarely other teachers in class (unless one
genuinely adheres to a radical pedagogy whereby all learners
are simultaneously teachers). She is the only one bearing her
perspective on the pedagogical enterprise. She alone is charged
with certain responsibilities for the learning she hopes will take
place. Her relationship to the subject matter or task at hand is
also unique. By contrast, when she is in her office surrounded
by books and journals and websites, she is ironically in much
closer touch with a community of peers who speak her language and share her particular interests. Analogously, when
ministers step into a pulpit or youth group gathering or vestry
meeting, they can feel much more isolated than they do in their
studies, surrounded there as they are by the commentaries,
study guides, and blogs authored by their own colleagues in the
religious enterprise. These forms of communication essentially
create communities of exchange, even if invisible ones, connecting individual ministers. It is in times of ministry "out there"

in the church community that the minister can sometimes feel stranded. She is typically the only one bearing her particular understanding of and relationship to the ministry. Her role in it is not easily shared or replaced because her identity is special. The parallel to a teacher's pedagogical isolation, then, is the minister's ecclesiastical isolation—isolation by virtue of the collar or robe.

I do not mean to make an elitist claim here or to exacerbate the way the ordained are set apart from the nonordained. I am simply trying to describe the reality many ministers face. Even those with a low theology of ordination who affirm the ministry of all believers still know that their status and role cause them to be viewed differently within the church. Ministers are put on pedestals not of their own making or are held to different standards or simply have expectations cast on them by virtue of their being ministers. They have also been shaped by years of formation and immersion in kinds of theological discourse that others in their communities simply have not experienced. Again, ironically, ministers search for conversation partners not only in the more scholarly activities of ministry but also when they are challenged, say, by disgruntled parishioners or dysfunctional committees or frustrating denominational structures. Everyday moments like these challenge a minister's sense of self and even theology. They can render it hard for us to make sense of what is happening to us. We can turn to parishioners in such times, of course, but our colleagues often more readily get it.

I would guess that many ministers fresh out of seminary do not envision this kind of loneliness. It is difficult to imagine not having peers around when one is a student in school (although part-time and commuting students can more easily imagine this, and a lot of seminarians can remember feelings of being stranded when they were adjusting to seminary at the start). Most of the students I work with anticipate that time management will be their biggest challenge in ministry, followed closely by the need for self-care. Their concern is to strike the right balance between the long hours they know they will have to spend alone preparing sermons and the equally long hours needed for visitation, committees, administration, and so on. If anything, they imagine isolation as simply one mode in which time gets spent, contrasted with the mode of frenetic busyness. What many of my students don't yet realize is that you can be busy and lonely at the same time. When you are the only one there like yourself, you can be surrounded by the company of others and be lonely. This is the loneliness of role, not surroundings. As a congregant who is also an ordained minister, for example, I have found that sometimes the pastors of the churches to which I belong have turned to me to share anecdotes or offer observations about the congregation, knowing that in me they have an understanding audience. I have stood in their shoes.

Shulman's answer to the problem of pedagogical isolation is to make teaching into "community property." If academics have lots of structured venues for talking with colleagues about their scholarship and fewer for talking about what is going on in their classrooms, then more venues for discussions about classroom teaching need to be created, he argues. Teachers need ways to turn to their colleagues for conversation, feedback, and assistance on the enterprise of teaching. "We don't judge each other's research on the basis of casual conversations in the hall; we say to our colleagues, 'That's a lovely idea! You really must write it up.'"[4] And so he suggests that academics stop relegating discussions about teaching to casual hallway chats between classes, as they so often do, and start taking their work *as teachers* as seriously as they do their scholarship. This is the only way they will receive thoughtful and intentional feedback about classroom life. It is the only way to create a culture wherein teaching is valued.

I like the image of ministry as community property. It has the potential to revolutionize the church the way Shulman envisions revolutionizing the academy. Peer groups are one way to make ministry community property. They are intentionally created spaces for sharing thoughts and feelings about what is going on in the ministries of individual ministers. Beyond that, they are venues for "writing up" ideas, trading best practices, exploring new developments. In them members find a supportive venue for talking about what it means to occupy the role of minister (in a world where that role sometimes feels like it is changing all the time). A peer group is one place where your ministry is rendered less isolating because it is shared, examined, and owned, at least for the moment, by a group of your sympathetic colleagues. I will say more in the next chapter about the specific ways colleagues in peer groups can engage each other in conversation about ministry, but suffice it here to say that any group should incorporate some process that lets members bring their experiences before the group for serious reflection. Ministers no longer need to suffer alone in silence— and if peer groups become standard and universal practice in the ministry, there will no longer be any excuse, either.

MANAGING THE DIFFICULTY OF MINISTRY

If pastors need to gain a better grasp on why their vocation is lonely, they also need to understand why it is so difficult. Several factors render the ordained ministry a difficult profession. To compare ministry once again to writing, some of the obvious difficulties are the same as those writers complain about. Like the writing life, the material rewards of the pastoral life tend to be slim. Few people will make it rich in either of these professions, even after toiling for many years. Required therefore is a sense of calling that transcends financial reward, often captured in the familiar advice only to accept a call to ministry "if you can't imagine doing anything else" (advice given, incidentally, to budding academics as well). Neither do many people become famous as writers or pastors. The same could probably be said of the greatest pastor alive today. Beyond that, the realities of ministry (like writing) today may require new practitioners to be flexible in their call. Fewer full-time positions exist these days, and an increasing number of ministers are supporting themselves financially, as many writers and academics have always done, by working second jobs. And finally, along with writers, ministers have it hard precisely because others think their craft comes easily. The cliche in the ministry world, of course, is that ministers work only one hour a week. Few parishioners—let alone people outside the church—have any accurate sense of the way ministers spend the working hours not connected to the one hour of worship where they can see the fruits of pastoral labor. Nobody has any idea, preachers complain, of how many hours go into producing a sermon, just as few of us have any idea of how much work it takes to write a novel. The final product seems so effortless, and all the more so the better the practitioner.

No wonder ministers need a place to go where they can whine a bit! When they gather in private, pastors do spend "a certain amount of time buzzing about how unbelievably, monumentally difficult [ministry] is," as Cunningham says. But to turn serious, ministry *is* difficult. Ministers are correct to identify the magnitude of difficulty in their work; when they talk about how hard it is, they are not merely bellyaching. Several things make ministry uniquely difficult. One set of authors says the problem lies in the complexity of the role: "Clergy have one of the most complex and daunting leadership roles of any professional. They are answerable to a whole congregation of people who have divergent views about what the leader ought to be doing. Their days are unpredictable because so many people have direct access to them. They lead a volunteer organization in which lay leaders flow in and out—constantly threatening organizational stability. Clergy leadership is an acid test for any leadership approach."[5] The ministry is surely a prime example of a professional role that is very complex. Many professions are characterized by complexity, but most ministers, especially in congregations, have never become specialized the way other professionals have, so they still have all these varied roles to play. There is truth to the claim, after all, that ministers are among the last generalists left in the professional world, and generalists are not always recognized for their mastery of difficult work the way specialists are. Add to that all the changes to religious life wrought by the postmodern era, and this generalist profession is rendered even more daunting. Being a leader in a radically changing landscape is not easy.

The above quote also alludes to the difficulty of church politics. Ministers have to answer to their congregations and, for those in hierarchical institutions, to superiors like bishops. Finally, the ministry has always been difficult if only because its central mission—whether you call it repairing the world or proclaiming the good news—is unarguably one of the hardest things God asks us to do. One pastor and theologian is even willing to call it "impossible." He writes, "What if the beginning of wisdom, and for that matter, the beginning of effective and faithful ministry, is to confess that ministry is quite simply impossible? And what if this is absolutely not an excuse, not a clever lowering of expectations that allows us to avoid giving it the good old college try? What if it's simply the truth? And what if embracing this truth is not only the beginning of wisdom, but also the beginning of faithful and effective leadership?"[6]

What can peer groups provide to gird pastors in the face of ministry's difficulty? The difficulty combined with the isolation of ministry *can* make its practitioners feel crazy, as though no one else in the world has ever gone through what they are going through. A pastor can face situations that are genuinely unique, so that every once in a while it may be true that even no other pastor has faced the same exact situation. But most of the time you are not alone in what you are experiencing. Peer groups, most basically, provide a measure of relief to you, especially if you are new: finally you know it's not about you! Groups provide some vindication from others who understand because they have lived through the same things. They become a venue for beginning to seek wisdom and perspective, not just tips and survival advice, about the difficulty of the calling.

Tim Dolan calls this "sense making." After studying several clergy clusters in Washington State, he concluded, "One major benefit of the clergy cluster was helping these pastors make sense of their lives and ministries in an increasingly complex and chaotic world. So many pastors *do* ministry, but so often have little opportunity to step back and reflect on—and make sense of—what it is they are doing."[7] For Dolan, peer group learning has proven noticeably different from some of the other forms of continuing education he has led in his career. A peer group often provides more sustained personal transformation of practitioners than do one-time conferences and programs that clergy attend on their own and then go home. The occasional continuing education event may provide a brief sense of solidarity and an infusion of new ideas into a minister's practice but does not necessarily provide an anchor amidst its complexity and difficulty.

This is not to say that peer groups automatically transform ministers' attitudes toward ministry. Some clergy are reluctant to join a group because, in their experience, such groups just provide an excuse to whine. Even in my own experience with student interns, I have seen it can be hard to stave off the belly-aching. Members of groups sometimes seem to want to one-up each other with their tales of misery. I believe one reason for this phenomenon is that we have precious few other models available to us besides the gripe session. Positive experiences of transformation through collegiality are unfortunately rare for many of us. For one thing, the educational systems through which most of us have been raised reinforce critique rather than mutual support. I think this teaches us to tear apart our experiences and each other's as well, rather than build them up. But another part of the problem is simply the litany of clergy woe that all of us have learned to recite. Like Cunningham's writer peers, the story of how monumentally difficult our profession becomes a familiar trope. We become like the stereotype of men and women in old age who can barely talk about anything besides their joint pain. All conversation somehow ends up being about the difficulty of our job.

But a peer group can become a place where we learn to sing a new song. By sharing problems with each other in a reflective way, clergy can access a perspective on their work they may not have known they had and thus make sense of the complex challenges their ministry presents. The most successful groups not only make space for admitting the genuine difficulty of the profession but also encourage the telling of a different story, one of excitement and joy in ministry. And if not that, at least a story that tells the truth about the hope that lies in ministry, even if it is an "impossible" one. Peer groups can also bring discernible hope to ministry leadership and practice. There is growing anecdotal if not hard evidence to suggest that peer groups have kept some ministers from leaving the ministry. Longtime clergy educator Bruce Roberts quotes one pastor in his research into the effect of clergy peer groups who admitted, "I probably wouldn't still be in my congregation if I wasn't able to come here and vent, and also rediscover that I'm not always crazy— that I can rediscover . . . the courage to go with my insight and use my gifts even though they weren't always well received by everybody."[8] Roberts used this pastor's testimony as an example of the way belonging to a group changes ministry practice.

For in the end, it is true that at least some ministers must be happy and hopeful in their ministries. As Cunningham says about writers, we must be acquainted with happiness or else we could not describe it and lead others to it.[9] I believe that more and more ministers are joyful and that their peers are helping them unearth that joy and use it to construct a counternarrative. Who knows? We might even become a witness to other professionals who labor without much reward!

CLAIMING AUTHENTICITY IN MINISTRY

A third reality that ministers today must grapple with is the need to stay *authentic*. Ministers have for so long been expected to be faultless—even in realms lying outside their ministerial work—and this sometimes leads them to try to be people they are not. Many especially feel as though they should be the superheroes of the faith. Someone once coined the phrase "super Christian" to denote a religious leader's responsibility to be the perfect human being. (After all, it is not only children who sometimes mistake clergy for God.) In the face of such an unrealistic expectation, ministers have often cowered. And yet I believe clergy dearly desire to be more themselves, less what others might want them to be. I find today's rising generation of ministers, in particular, to be generally less tolerant when others cast unreasonable expectations on them, and I celebrate this trend. Safe collegial settings, in which they can be candid about their experience, help a great deal. Simply put, authentic sharing with other pastors can lead to more authenticity in the practice of ministry. Pastors no longer have to pretend to be all things to all people and can be more truly themselves.

But where did the pressure to be inauthentic come from in the first place? I would argue that ministers have typically felt, in particular, a burden to be experts in all things theological and spiritual. As Roman Catholic moral theologian Richard Gula puts it: "Through diverse functions, pastoral ministers serve as a theological resource for the community by lifting up and living out the word. We are recognized as the ones trained to discern meaning by being both reliable interpreters of the stories of God's presence and action in the world and witnesses to them."[10] In my own work, I have written that clergy face pressure to *have the answers and to say the right things.* "Clergy are made to think their role is to make the faith clear and accessible, to win people to it, and that to them alone falls the task of being an apologist for it."[11] But the mysteries of faith are often just that: mysteries. Faith is not always clear. Nevertheless, clergy sometimes find it difficult to know how to respond to the pressure put upon them to make the mysterious clear and the complex simple. They feel burdened and even frightened, because when they don't have the answers, they can start to question themselves and their own spiritual maturity. Some compensate by sounding more confident than they really feel, talking in a way that sounds more certain than they know the answers to be.

At the risk of sounding blasphemous, I have given a name to this phenomenon of overcompensation: ecclesial bullshit. Bullshit is a style of self-representation that falls just short of outright lying but that blurs truth and falsity. It seeks to create an impression of confidence when confidence is actually lacking. Sometimes it seeks to impress. When you resort to this way of being pastoral, let's face it, you are trying to snow the other person. Your listener doesn't know any better than you what is theologically or spiritually true or false, and so you try to take advantage of the ambiguity by getting them not to assess truth and falsity too closely. Instead you steer them toward a comforting, reasonable-sounding interpretation of God's actions that will satisfy both of you.

Eventually most people see through the snow that is bullshit. They realize what they are hearing: an attempt on the part of the one talking to prop himself up. In the end, therefore, the damage done by bullshit is not just that theological convictions are made up but also that would-be theological experts get exposed as frauds. The community then withdraws the trust it bestowed. This is why bullshit is so pernicious in the ministry. It tarnishes the trust between ministers and those they minister to. While parishioners' expectations may be unreasonable at times, they do justifiably turn to their pastors to help them comprehend things that are incomprehensible, like the death of a child. In the end, they want honesty as much as certainty, and bullshit denies them both. I believe that what the majority of people in congregations really seek in their leaders is not so much expertise in all things, but rather an honest and dedicated commitment to searching always for meaning. They want to have their own incomprehension honored and taken seriously. Some people may want all the mysteries cleared up, but most want someone by their side who will accompany them as they venture into the unknown territories of their faith.

To give ministers the benefit of the doubt, I acknowledge that they often resort to bullshit when they desperately need to fake their way through a situation more complex than they wish it were. Bullshit is an attempt at preserving authority. It may even represent an ironic attempt to preserve authenticity. But as John Wimmer of the Lilly Endowment's Sustaining Pastoral Excellence program has said, "Pastors do not have all the answers, and acting as if they do could be one of the biggest enemies of pastoral excellence." How can peers help? Peer groups can help cut through pastoral bullshit. Wimmer sees great potential in a peer group model that helps save ministers from having to be know-it-alls. "They can give up the facade of knowing it all and become listeners who empower the laity and awaken their gifts for ministry."[12] If the group is a good one, its members can come and admit with honesty the theological and pastoral answers they do not have. The group creates a space where ministers offer each other something besides easy solutions to the problems of ministry. Simply put, when group members do not tolerate bullshit from each other, the facade of pastoral perfection can be dropped. Pastors can become themselves.

Dolan offers a more sophisticated explanation for what peer groups achieve in this regard by referencing the psychological notion of the holding environment. Originally used to describe the mother-child bond, then applied to the therapeutic relationship, Dolan (and others) use the concept to describe any setting where people are held in a supportive relationship that allows them to share on a deep and personal level and thus find protection for their fears and concerns. Holding environments "put appropriate boundaries on people's anxiety and help regulate the distress people feel when they are being stretched to make challenging adjustments in their lives." Dolan found when he interviewed pastors who had participated in peer groups that they all found their peer groups to be safe and supportive places where they could "process their lives and their ministries."[13]

In their book *Know Your Story and Lead with It*, pastors and teachers Richard L. Hester and Kelli Walker-Jones describe the peer groups they created in North Carolina. They believed it was vitally important for clergy to have a place to go to learn to tell their authentic stories. To achieve this, they adopted for these groups the rule from Parker Palmer's practice of Circles of Trust: "No fixing, no saving, no advising, no setting each other straight."[14] Hester and Walker-Jones insisted that instead of being the place where ministers go to get quick fixes to their problems or tips to apply back home, a peer group should focus on listening, probing, and questioning. While difficult to practice because countercultural, this rule proved important for generating the right environment for authenticity. Saving the other members of the group from their errors is a tempting practice, but it only reinforces the sense that you should be perfect as a minister (or else you wouldn't make an *error*). Fixing problems also contributes to the idea that perfection is desired. Even advising, which seems like such a normal activity for a group of peers, implies that right ways and wrong ways to handle situations in ministry can be identified and codified. A discipline of listening without fixing, saving, or advising creates instead an attitude of support, openness, and inquiry. It leaves open the possibility that something new might always emerge from the person telling their story. This, in turn, reinforces the idea that there is rarely one right answer to the problems in ministry.

Hester and Walker-Jones believe strongly in the "power of not-knowing." By this they mean the power that comes from openness to multiple interpretations of reality. Not-knowing requires a determined effort not to impose one version of the truth on others or oneself. "Many people and groups try to impose their narratives on ministers. The constant pressure to live into the preferred stories of others can be disorienting."[15] Peer groups can encourage a culture of not-knowing, and thus authenticity, by creating space for telling multiple stories about life and about ministry. In the process, a liberated pastoral identity can emerge. And, I might add, it strikes me that clergy who have successfully learned in a peer group not to fix, save, advise, or set each other straight might be able to avoid these behaviors with parishioners as well. In the end, clergy participation in peer groups could ultimately be a gift to congregations, because of the way these groups help to create a culture of authenticity that can spread throughout entire communities.

A New Type of Ministerial Formation

While peer groups are about helping pastors face the realities of ministry today, they are also about creating a new way of *learning* to be a pastor. I now look at peer groups from the perspective of how they are changing the nature and practice of clergy formation. If you are a new pastor reading this book, I hope these ideas will encourage you to make a habit of turning to your peers, for you can learn a lot from them, especially under the right circumstances. As James P. Wind and David J. Wood write about clergy who are transitioning into ministry, "*How* one learns ministry in these early years is as important as *what* one learns. . . . If the initial experience of being a novice is generative, it sets the stage for embracing the need for learning that one encounters in the course of a lifetime of ministry."[16] Even if you are not new to ministry, and whether or not your early experiences generated a bounty of learning, changing the way you approach your formation could help change your experience. Peer groups are a great example of the sort of formation that can be resumed at any time after formal schooling is over. Their power can be explained by referring to two theories about learning and formation—the concept of the "reflective practitioner" and that of the "community of practice."

REFLECTIVE PRACTITIONERS

The idea that good professionals are those who become *reflective practitioners* can be traced back to the work of engineer and educator Donald Schon, who for many years was a professor at the Massachusetts Institute of Technology. His books *The Reflective Practitioner: How Professionals Think in Action* and *Educating the Reflective Practitioner*, published during the 1980s, are still influential. Schon's central conviction is that there are excellent practitioners across all professions whose excellence shares something in common: They possess a certain kind of knowledge, a way of knowing, that is really best described as a kind of artistry. He called this reflection-in-action. It involves the art of learning by doing, a skill that enables professionals to tap into what they instinctively know how to do but haven't always put into words. The same skill helps them share their know-how with others. I focus on reflection-in-action, because it is in many ways the very skill or art that peer groups surface.

Schon's interest in "how professionals think in action" began when he noticed a widespread crisis in confidence in professionalism. It seemed that many people had lost faith in the way professionals were being prepared. Despite their having completed sophisticated degree programs in education, law, and business, it appeared that teachers couldn't teach, lawyers couldn't lawyer, and MBAs couldn't run businesses. Why was professional education supposedly failing in its mission? Schon did not think practitioners were getting dumber or educators necessarily getting worse, so there had to be another explanation. Schon's answer lay in a flaw at the heart of professional formation. Its primary model assumed that practitioners acquired a lot of theoretical knowledge during school that they then *applied* to their practice. (He called this the technical rationality model.) So, engineers learned physics and applied it to building bridges, psychotherapists read Freud and applied it to their patients, and so on. (As far as I know, Schon never directly investigated theological education, but a similar pattern could be discerned there: seminarians learn Bible, theology, and history and apply what they learn to the practice of ministry.) At its best, this model assumed that as problems arose in professional practice, they could be taken to academics, who would supply the "pure" knowledge that could eventually be applied to solving the problems.

The problem with this model was twofold. First, it led to a gap between the supposedly rigorous academic knowledge that schools supplied and the supposedly relevant practical application that professionals carried out. We become aware of this gap when researchers in the academy feel they have less and less to say directly to practitioners who don't seem to be listening to what they say anyway. We notice it when practitioners protest that they graduate from school, get out into the field, and discover that what they learned in the classroom hasn't prepared them for "the real world."

But the theory-to-practice model also seriously underestimates the intellectual work that practitioners are engaged in all the time (even though they may not call it "intellectual work"). The second problem with the model is the way it obscures the unique knowledge professionals possess that is different from the knowledge cultivated through book learning and pure research. To take just one example, a pastor may be faced with a tough committee meeting where Mrs. X can't stop pouting about how the confirmands behaved in church last week. As he listens to her, it dawns on him that the youths' behavior was not awful but simply reflected the cultural conditioning of a different generation. Having assessed the crux of the problem, he can sympathize with Mrs. X but still skillfully transform the tone of the meeting from one of despair into hope. He may have once read an article on generational differences, but the point is that he was engaged in real intellectual work during that meeting that transcended simply remembering and applying something he read.

What Schon decided to do was study the know-how that really good professionals display. He wanted to examine very closely the artistry of their practice in order to figure out the ingredients of exceptionally competent practice. What, exactly, goes into "a feel for the music" that enables great jazz musicians to improvise? The intuition that helps the top diagnosticians recognize when a patient is suffering from more than one disease at the same time? Today we might ask what kind of savvy the great church leaders have who not only can keep their congregations going but also can anticipate the emerging needs of congregations in the future. Can this knowledge be unearthed and shared? Schon drew upon scientist and philosopher Michael Polanyi's notion of tacit knowledge to describe what he was after.

In brief, what Schon hit upon was the idea that good practitioners don't just learn theories or rules and *then* act on them; they figure out what's going on *while* engaged in action. Hence, *reflection-in-action*. The exceptional practitioner can quite quickly notice when something goes unusually wrong (or surprisingly right) in the midst of their practice. They can then respond to the surprise by pondering what happened, questioning their assumption, and improvising a response. They do this all without even noticing what they are doing. Sometimes the process happens quickly, as in the example of our pastor rescuing a committee meeting gone bad, and sometimes slowly, as when a rector adjusts her leadership style as her parish grows from pastoral to program size. Though a tacit process, good practitioners can usually articulate afterward, in a sort of Monday morning quarterbacking way, what they did and how.

Schon writes that we shouldn't be surprised that professionals have these hidden smarts. "Phrases like 'thinking on your feet,' 'keeping your wits about you,' and 'learning by doing' suggest not only that we can think about doing but that we can think about doing something while doing it."[17] Nevertheless, two elements of reflection-in-action turn out to be key, and they are principles that can guide any practitioner who wants to get better at doing what he or she does. First, unfamiliar, novel situations trigger a practitioner's know-how. Second, other people, such as colleagues and coaches, are integral to reflection. Good practice, and reflection on practice, isn't carried out alone. Indeed, these principles guided Schon's recommendations for professional education and they are directly relevant to our interest in peer groups. Practitioners benefit significantly from having a regular context (the studio, the master class, the supervision session), he argued, to which they can bring a problem or situation from their practice and where they can hash it out with others in order to discover what they already know, find out what others know, and engage in reflection that challenges routine assumptions and encourages improvisation.

I have often said that a high level of competence in ministry practice is a good thing, and I am glad that there are lots of effective pastors out there. But so, too, is the ability to reflect on the meaning(s) of competent ministry. Too often this ability is perfected only in those who are privileged enough to have the time to read and write. Being able to reflect well *on* practice while engaged *in* practice is a truly valuable combination that many ministers sadly lack the opportunity to develop. If peer groups can help develop more reflective practitioners, that will be a very good thing.

COMMUNITIES OF PRACTICE

While peer groups represent a venue for producing reflective practitioners, they also represent an example of the *communities of practice* that are increasingly recognized as an important venue in which practitioners of all sorts learn to hone their crafts. Basically, communities of practice are gatherings of people, like ministers, who share a passion for what they do and want to get better at it by exchanging ideas and supporting one another on an ongoing basis. Communities of practice can be formal or informal. Sometimes we may not even realize we are part of one. Leading thinkers on this phenomenon, Etienne Wenger, Richard McDermott, and William M. Snyder, offer as examples the clusters of engineers in Silicon Valley who exchange design ideas, groups of soccer moms who trade tips on parenting, artists who gather in cafes to argue over emerging styles, even members of urban gangs who initiate one another into the ways of street life.[18] Such communities all bring together like-minded people who share some interest and who support each other's individual pursuit of that interest. Members of communities of practice do not necessarily work or pursue their interests together. They all have jobs or lives of their own, but it is these jobs and lives that become the focus when they gather.

Wenger et al. draw upon many of the ideas we find in Schon. They are very interested in the nature of knowledge and how it gets produced and managed within organizations. They talk about the organic, lively nature of knowledge and how it "lives in the human act of knowing. If a friend told you that he had read many books about surgery and was ready to operate on your skull, you would be right to decline politely.

When surgeons operate on a patient, they do not blindly apply knowledge they have gleaned from books or procedures they have stored in their heads."[19] They acknowledge, after Polanyi, that much practical knowledge tends to remain tacit and undocumented, unlike other kinds of knowledge. Tacit knowledge requires informal and subtle means for accessing it, "such as storytelling, conversation, coaching and apprenticeship."[20] Knowledge is also relational. Coming primarily from the business world, they appreciate how it gets embodied in people, not texts or tools, and can get lost in many businesses, where people are sometimes prevented from interacting because they get trapped in the silos created by managerial and bureaucratic structures. This is where communities of practice come in. Communities of practice cut across traditional structures like teams or staffing units (denominations?) and can therefore help "steward" knowledge.[21]

Wenger et al. identify three elements of any community of practice: domain, community, and practice. The *domain*, or domain of inquiry, is the organizing discourse or area of expertise around which your community gathers. It's the answer to the question "What is your group about?" or "What do you talk about each month?" or even "Why do you hang out with those people all the time?" In the ministry, it might be something like "the problems we face as leaders of small membership churches in Nebraska" or "how the liberation theology I learned in seminary is relevant to my ministry today." Identifying the domain lets members know what problems and questions to bring to the group. Occasionally, the actual domain is different from the official one. Wenger et al. give the example of a group of medical insurance claims processors who ostensibly gather to share ideas about how to meet their quotas but who really share strategies for surviving in such a difficult job.[22] In the professional guild to which I belong, it took me only one meeting to realize that while I would gain some practical ideas by attending each year, I would also learn from my peers how to deal with the shared phenomenon of marginalization within our institutions.

Community is not a difficult concept for ministers of the church to understand. It's the glue that holds the group together, the collective relationships that form the body. It is not important that community members all hold exactly the same position in their institutions or possess the same level of expertise or have been members of the group for the same length of time, but they should be expected to contribute to building wisdom about the domain. Several considerations enter into selecting community members and maintaining health communities; I will discuss these in the next chapter.

Practice refers to the approaches, techniques, styles, and accepted standards that the members of the community use in their work. It's best thought of in the plural, as in "best practices." Identifying the practices you share in your day-to-day work will help you plan what kinds of activities you will engage in when you gather as a group. In the context of ministry, *practices* would refer to disciplines like theological reflection and spiritual practices. A clergy peer group learns together how to do these things better.

In the end, the three elements of domain, community, and practice are inseparable and interrelated. They all help define the purpose of the group. All three need attention, for a well-defined community flourishes. Of particular concern for clergy may be striking the right balance between the importance of community and the importance of practice. I will say more about this in the next chapter, but as Wenger et al. point out, "a community that does not develop a shared practice will remain a diffuse friendship group that may be socially satisfying, but ineffective."[23]

Let me give two examples from my own life of what I have later come to realize were communities of practice I belonged to. They both come from the time when I was enrolled in a doctoral program, but they could equally have arisen in a nonacademic setting. My first example is of potluck dinners. The doctoral students in our program would get together in each other's homes about once a month for a potluck. Ostensibly, these gatherings were purely for fellowship; we had other venues for sharing our scholarship with each other and engaging in substantive discussion. But the dinners were very formative in their own way. Looking back, I realize that they helped me understand what it meant to be a doctoral student and a member of the wider academic community. A fifth-year student might come back from a job interview and tell the rest of us what questions the search committee had asked. A first-year might query the group as to what texts the professors would expect her already to have read. Always there was talk about how to survive the dissertation years and speculation about the myths and realities of what the academic job market might offer us. Advice and mutual support were freely shared at those potlucks, but beyond advice we received an enculturation into what it meant to be a budding academic.

Another example comes from my last two years in the program. I found that I wanted support from other women writing dissertations on feminist topics, so I formed a writing group that met biweekly to read drafts of each other's work. The group was formed by invitation, and we set some basic rules for participation, but it was informal in the sense of existing (as did the potluck dinners) outside any formal institutional structures. Members did not even come from the same academic departments. During the years that group met, I never ceased to be amazed at the willingness of five women to take the time away from their own writing to read material from far outside their own fields, just to help someone else become a better writer. We became a tight group. We learned to offer critique in a way that could be heard. We learned not to let each other off the hook. (One of the rules was you had to bring something to the group if it was your turn. A page of notes or an outline was all right, but it had to advance your writing project.) We learned a lot about how writers in other disciplines approach writing. We also commiserated over difficult advisors and the challenges to surviving graduate school. To this day I credit that group for helping me complete my dissertation and the degree itself.

Ministry peer groups, properly constituted, are an example of communities of practice. Whether you gather for a specific purpose, such as coaching each other through projects, or for more general support, you will be contributing to each other's formation as ministers. A peer group is a community of practice if the focus is on building community and reflecting on practice. There are, after all, other sorts of gatherings of ministers that might not necessarily be considered communities of practice. The ecumenical clergy group in town that gathers once a month to hear a speaker talk to them about some current program or project is not really a community of practice. The group of pastors who get together monthly to study the lectionary texts may or may not be one. Certainly denominational committees and other groups charged with purely administrative tasks are not. The "lunch bunch" of clergy who meet at the local diner for breakfast every Thursday to exchange gossip and news is not a community of practice. It's not that communities of practice have to be formal, but they do have to be intentional. They are not so much about trying to complete something together as about supporting each other's development. They encourage the formation of rather significant relationships. Members' focus is on each other and what each one is doing and trying to accomplish. Members are committed to each other and each other's growth as practitioners.

COMMUNITIES OF LEARNING

Lee Shulman, whose work we encountered earlier, uses the same idea of communities of practice to promote new approaches to education. His approaches are relevant to our discussion of clergy peer groups insofar as their goal is the continuing education and formation of ministers. He writes about "communities of learners" and argues that four principles characterize contexts where learners become genuine allies of each other. As he puts it, these four principles describe the "conditions for effective, substantive, and enduring learning."[24] Shulman's primary context is the elementary school classroom, but I borrow his convictions to fit adult learning contexts as well, including peer groups. First, communities of learning encourage active as opposed to passive ways of learning. Real work can be said to be going on. (This is why I said that a news-and-gossip clique was not a community of practice.) In the peer reflection groups (Practicum) I led, the best days were ones when students stopped merely swapping anecdotes and started really trying to figure out some aspect of the ministerial role. I remember one discussion about whether professional ministry was a *job*, a *career*, or a *calling* during which students arrived at a consensus that creatively combined aspects of each. (They felt genuinely called to the work but were unwilling to sacrifice some of the practical considerations about just compensation and boundaries associated with jobs, for example, and some of the positive aspects of ambition that they had come to appreciate from their own experiences in nonministry careers.) In fact, creative thinking resulted from their own refusal to select among the forced choices I, the teacher, had given them. They were, indeed, actively defining what ministry meant to them.

Second, in communities of learning, members engage each other on a level beyond mere reception and exchange of information and ideas. They can actually reflect on *how* they came to know what they know. Shulman calls this "going meta." He talks about groups that use written cases as a basis for discussion and how even identifying what constitutes a case is itself an interesting discussion.[25] Indeed, we used to spend a fair amount of time getting students in Practicum to reflect on the nature of the cases they had written up. We asked individual case writers why they had brought forth the ones they did. We also asked the whole group to articulate all the things a particular case might be a case *of* and not only what it was *about*. For example, a case about a couple with no ties to the church asking to be married could be seen as a case of ministerial authority, of evangelizing the unchurched, of the meaning of church weddings—and so on. Students then had to articulate what they thought about, say, the parameters of ministerial authority and why they thought that way. Students' ability to "go meta" with cases and engage them on this level elevated the discussion beyond "What would you do if you were the minister in this situation?" What-would-you-do discussions are a very tempting way for a group to work, but they only invite group members to fix each other's problems. While having some value in the short run, fixing problems is not the same thing as generating knowledge. In a genuine community of learning, you want to understand why the other people in your group think about situations the way they do—where they are coming from. This gives you insight into their perspective, their theology, and their sense of ministerial identity, which in turn invites constructive reflection on the meanings of ministry that the case has provoked you to grapple with. You cannot do this intellectual work unless you "go meta."

Third, in communities of learners, learners collaborate by working together. As Shulman puts it, one student's learning *scaffolds* the others'.[26] I saw this scaffolding going on all the time in my Practicum groups, typically occurring when two students from very different ministry settings would discover that they had significantly different takes on a situation. Rather than just argue with each other, they were encouraged to explain how their respective contexts mattered to their respective interpretations. For example, one time we were discussing ministry to people living with mental illness, which led to a debate about how our society provides mental health care. One intern in a congregational setting argued that the (over)professionalization of secular services in our society indicates a lack of

confidence in communities of faith as caregivers to the suffering. She suspected that the creation of so many specialties
within health care only served the health care industry, not necessarily the patients, who needed caring communities. But another intern, who was working in a locked psychiatric ward of
a mental health hospital and certainly saw more professionals
than he could have ever imagined parading through to serve a
small number of patients, described to his classmate how des-
perate and severe the patients' conditions were. He explained
that he had come to realize from firsthand experience how important it was that a safety net was in place for them and that
a good safety net required a highly specialized staff of mental
health professionals. At the same time, he himself could see the
need for congregations to be ready and able to receive former
patients after they were discharged from the hospital. In short,
these two students could teach each other out of their very different contexts, able to do so because they belonged to a peer
group that taught them to scaffold their learning.

Overcoming Resistance to Peer Group Learning

Peer groups are contributing in several important ways to new
models for clergy formation that are becoming increasingly vital today.[27] But a peer group is not necessarily an easy model to
put into practice. A genuine community of practice or community of learning can be challenging to generate and to maintain
precisely because it represents a departure from traditional approaches to formation. New habits take time to develop. So I
conclude this chapter with an honest examination of the skep-
ticism some people bring to belonging to a peer group and ways
to overcome that.

   If peer groups are so promising, why hasn't everybody
jumped on the peer group bandwagon? What makes forming
and sustaining a peer group hard? Why do so many of us still
think we can only learn how to do ministry by going to seminars

and conferences or pursuing advanced degrees? After all, most of us have had numerous experiences of attending conferences where we have sat quietly by ourselves in a large room listening to an expert speak at us from a microphone, taking notes that we bring home, put in a file, and never read again. Why do we repeat such experiences?

Well, first, peer groups represent but one type of formation. They don't accomplish everything. For one thing, they typically cannot provide a venue for hearing about the latest research or emerging theories in the field. In general, they are not as good at covering content, and sometimes content is precisely what we need to learn. In this regard, learning from experts will always have a place. The previous discussions about collaborative peer learning and tacit knowledge notwithstanding, some topics are just better presented by one person "in the know" who talks to the rest. Frankly, there are some things that I wouldn't want to try to understand by listening to my peers' stories. (Clergy income tax comes to mind.) Sometimes the traditional mode of learning whereby knowledge is transmitted from teacher to student is not only efficient but also preferable.

Expertise is inspiring, moreover, and what experts have to say compels us the way our peers sometimes do not. Leaders in their field have invested a great deal of time and thought, after all, in what they teach us. I remember sitting through a course in graduate school where the professor, committed to communities of learning, had us create our own class presentations based on the primary theological texts we had read. At the end of each session he might weigh in with his own interpretation, but his reflections were usually brief. I found myself itching to hear more from him and less from my fellow students. I even remember thinking, "I didn't pay tuition to learn from people just as clueless as I am about what all this stuff means!" When it comes to learning some material, we need and deserve the wisdom of those who have dedicated their lives to its study. So I would be the last person to say that traditional teaching and scholarship have no place in learning and that everything we need to understand about ministry we can gain through participation in a peer group.

A community-of-practice approach to learning is also hard because it is less controlled and controllable. The kind of groups I have been describing—no lesson plan or teacher or text or even formal presentation—by nature tends to be somewhat disorderly. You never know what people are going to say or what direction the discussion is going to take. Even Lee Shulman jokes about the classroom he envisions and his own principles about learning: "If you take these principles seriously, and you imagine what a classroom would look like, in which activity, reflection, collaboration, passion, generativity and community were going on at the same time, you would likely have what you call in Hebrew a *balagan*, a chaotic mess."[28] And he was still envisioning a proper classroom with a teacher! Ministry peer groups can be even messier. I was once part of a denominational clergy group that met to do theological reflection, and I will never forget the day a colleague of mine attended for his first (and last) time. I knew by the way the discussion unfolded that he would never be back. It was simply too random for him, as everyone wanted to talk about different things, and did. I stuck it out longer, because I always left the group stretched theologically, but only after accepting the fact that the experience would be a bit of a *balagan*.

A final challenge is that, frankly, learning from experience is exceedingly difficult. It can seem on the surface like a lot of storytelling and anecdote swapping. I sometimes fretted that my students in Practicum weren't really learning anything. It was difficult to point to particular lessons that had been instilled in them or skills they had acquired by talking to each other for an hour and a half a week about their internships, and as a teacher I wanted to see such progress happening. I wanted evidence that my interns were better ministers at the end of the year for having taken Practicum, and this was hard to come by. At one teachers' meeting at the end of an academic year, I anxiously pressed the teachers to prove to me some way that the students in their groups were smarter about ministry than they had been at the beginning of the year. Finally, one of them gently pointed out to me that I should take my own teaching philosophy seriously. If I really subscribed to the theory that experiences in ministry themselves generate reflective learning, then I had to accept that learning would ultimately become evident only in the course of *future experiences*. Proof of intellectual growth wouldn't come in the form of "lessons" learned, but that didn't mean students hadn't gotten smarter. They would find themselves two years after graduation putting something they learned in Practicum into practice. I would most likely never become aware of the connection, and even they might not detect it. My teacher wisely reminded me that when it comes to this sort of education and formation, we must remain confident that we are planting seeds whose fruit will be borne out eventually. In the end, we are hoping to develop a *kind* of practitioner more than a concrete set of practical skills and lessons.

Those who participate in peer groups have to exercise the same patience that I learned to develop as a teacher of Practicum. Members may initially feel like little gets accomplished in them. Referring to my dissertation group, in fact, I realize I did not really see marked improvement in my writing until several years after the group ceased meeting. But I know I took away from it some habits and disciplines that surely contributed to the way my writing got better. The best groups will feel worthwhile to their members even if none of them can articulate afterward what, precisely, they learned.

On a bit more theoretical level, communities of practice are challenging because of the kind of knowledge surfaced in them. What we are after, in clergy peer groups, remember, is how someone becomes an excellent, effective, and happy minister. This is harder than just knowing the right games to play with youth in confirmation class or remembering the sequence of Paul's journeys. Putting into words for your peers how your ministry is becoming more effective takes real intellectual work.

Imagine trying to explain, for example, how you revitalized your congregation, eased it through conflict, and stayed sane throughout. You would probably say something like "It just happened." I know, because I visited all the supervisors participating in my internship program and heard this all the time. Very typically, when I would ask what made ministry at their sites work, they would recite facts and figures about the programs going on there. (Or they would simply credit the Holy Spirit.) When I would press supervisors to tell me *how* and *why* the ministry programs were effective, they would often have a difficult time answering. This is why it's called tacit knowledge! Even a virtuoso violinist cannot explain how she plays Mozart so beautifully; she just *can*. As Schon recognized, excellent practitioners are not even always aware of their own excellence. But as Wenger et al. write, "The tacit aspects of knowledge are often the most valuable. They consist of embodied expertise— a deep understanding of complex, interdependent systems."[29]

Tacit knowledge emerges slowly. You have to hang out with a person for a long time and hear a lot of stories in order to pick up on all the clues that will eventually let you know how they learned to do what they can do. This is why soccer moms look for each other week after week in the bleachers, why artists frequent the same cafes, and why engineers cluster together at all the professional meetings. Learning important things from your peers takes time and patience. Ultimately, after all, it is the practitioners themselves who embody the knowledge. Without knowing *them*, you will never really understand their practice.

CLERGY PEER GROUPS HAVE THE POTENTIAL to transform both individual ministers and the way ministers are formed for their work. They are not a magic bullet that will in and of itself eliminate the loneliness, difficulty, and pressures of the profession, but they can ameliorate these conditions. In the next chapter, we will look more closely at how they operate.

4

Community Property: Peer Group Practice

IN THE PREVIOUS CHAPTER, I outlined the theories behind why peer groups are becoming so popular. This chapter is more practical. In it I will offer assistance and advice for readers who want to create or participate in a peer group. This chapter is organized around a set of questions and answers. Peer groups have been around long enough that a body of wisdom has been generated about what makes a group work. On the one hand, people who have studied these groups recognize there are many different types and that decisions about design will depend on the type of group desired. No one size fits all. On the other hand, they have also come to agree on certain principles and practices that seem to help groups operate at their best. This chapter is for readers who are thinking of starting or joining a peer group. I acknowledge that seminaries and judicatories often establish peer group programs and that as an individual minister you may not be in the position to start one from scratch. Nevertheless, the considerations raised in this chapter will still be relevant to your participation, whether or not you had a hand in creating your group. Ongoing ownership of and responsibility for a group by all its members are really what makes one succeed anyway.

Peer groups function in different ways. The term is an umbrella including the support group, the fellowship group, the best practices group, and the study group. There are groups that do fun things together, read books, invite guest speakers, or travel around the world on mission trips. For the purposes of this chapter, I have in mind groups that, whatever activities they engage in, function as a cross between a support group and a continuing education program. I define them as *intentional gatherings of ministers who come together voluntarily but regularly for the purpose of becoming better ministers.* This definition leaves room for a wide variety of pursuits and common interests. It does not preclude your focusing on a domain of inquiry such as rural church ministry or youth mentoring or feminist theology. But it draws your attention always toward learning how to improve one another's practice in the domain and support one another's formation for excellence. I draw here, as in the previous chapter, upon the concept of a *community of practice.*

Q: How do you present the idea to potential members?

If you share my basic understanding that your group is a community of practice for those who want to become better ministers, you will need to explain its purpose carefully up front. Many of the people you invite will have belonged to something in their lives that could have been called a community of practice, as my own experience shows, but they may have just called it a colleague group. They may not have appreciated how participation in the group was leading them to become a better something-or-other or even that there was any purpose at all to what they were doing. So while potential members may recognize what you are talking about, it is wise to be explicit. It is also important to make your implicit understandings explicit for the following reason: far more people have belonged to groups in their lives that were not communities of practice. People get asked to join gatherings of like-minded colleagues all the time. But usually there is either an agenda for which they are being recruited ("Join other clergy in the area who support low-income housing") or no agenda at all ("Join with other clergy under thirty to drink coffee, be there for each other, and talk about whatever's on our minds"). The former is not really about them at all; they are warm bodies enlisted for a cause, and becoming involved in such a group may or may not contribute to making their ministry stronger (though it can, and undoubtedly the cause is strengthened). The under-thirty clergy, in contrast, are all about each other, but the purpose of gathering over coffee is left so loosely defined that the promise of getting something out of the gathering is unclear. It runs the risk of becoming a mere social group. Because these sorts of experiences resonate in people's minds when they are approached to join a group, you will want to be as clear as possible about what you have in mind.

Q: What considerations should go into the design of a clergy peer group?

Several elements of the design of a peer group will make a difference as to how it functions. It's important to note up front, however, that peer groups are, as Wenger et al. put it, "living communities" and as such will change over time. You cannot simply create a group and expect it to be a finished product. Your members will have a voice in how your group develops, according to what is needful and meaningful to them. You will want to be open to elements that develop as the group takes shape. "The organic nature of communities of practice challenges us to design these elements with a light hand, with an appreciation that the idea is to create liveliness, not manufacture a predetermined outcome."[1]

If you are launching a group, however, you will want to give some thought to *who* will join and *why*. The two are interconnected. Identifying why your group is being created will inform who gets invited to it. Will this be a group for clergy from a certain geographical area? Those new to the ministry? Those serving large multistaff churches? Those interested in a certain topic? A group will last only as long as it retains its members' interests, so it's important to organize people not simply according to traditional groupings but always to consider, What is it that the clergy I know really care about? What problems or topics interest them enough to get them in a group? Will they share what they know with each other? Answering these questions will help you establish and communicate your basic intent and help you decide whom to invite.

Then, you will need to decide on *how many*, *when*, and *where*. It is difficult to say how large or small a clergy peer group should be. Size affects function, and yet many different sized groups have flourished in the past. You need a critical mass, because even with the most committed members, someone will miss a meeting occasionally. Of course, funding may dictate the answer to this question. How often will your group meet, and where? These decisions, too, will affect how your group develops and whether it succeeds. Meet too infrequently, and you run the risk of never developing cohesion as a community. Meet too frequently, though, and members may feel overburdened and start skipping meetings. As for location, is there a place that serves as a good central spot for everybody? Do you want to retreat to a lovely setting, even if this adds to the cost? Will you rotate among each other's workplaces? Generally, gathering in the same location provides consistency, yet you want to be fair to those who might have to travel long distances. Will you always meet in person and in real time? With possibilities expanding all the time for ways to meet virtually, you might consider teleconferencing, videoconferencing, webinars, or establishing an online community. These modes of meeting enable even ministers who live in low density areas to create peer groups. They can, of course, also supplement face-to-face experiences.

There is also the question of whether your group will be open or closed once it forms. Groups whose purpose requires a high level of interpersonal trust may want to close themselves to new members. But given the transience of many clergy, especially in certain parts of the country, you run the risk of a premature end when members depart the area or move on to different jobs. My dissertation writing group lost and gained members over the years, and I even remained involved for a while after I moved five hundred miles away, but we eventually dispersed when there were no longer enough of us still enrolled in school and living in town.

Finally, you will need to decide *what*, exactly, you will do at your meetings. This question is related to your domain, of course, but is more concrete. Do you want to organize learning activities? Share works in progress or cases? Practice a spiritual discipline? Undertake a project together? Take turns bringing questions and problems for discussion? A combination of these? Again, the group members will inevitably want to weigh in, and you may not want to do the same things all the time, but some attention ahead of time to what is expected will help potential members understand what is in it for them. I will turn now to questions of *what* and offer some suggestions; they occupy a central part of the rest of this chapter.

Q: Shouldn't we just be a sounding board for members to talk about the problems they face becoming better ministers?

A group bearing the marks of a community of practice will necessarily be about the common pursuit everyone is interested in that brings them together in the first place (called *the domain* in the previous chapter), in this case ministry or a certain kind of ministry. But organizing yourself exclusively around *problems* has three pitfalls (quite aside from the fact that it can get depressing). First, if your raison d'être is being a sounding board for members' problems, you will attract members who have problems. A peer group striving to be a community of practice is really not a support group for those struggling in ministry. If it becomes this, it will alienate clergy who are not struggling and who want to engage in stimulating and constructive conversation about their vocation. Clergy who need a lot of help are probably best advised to seek it elsewhere. You can subtly communicate this by emphasizing that this will be a group seeking to think hard and creatively about ministry.

Second, without correcting for it, a group can easily become focused on problems of the how-to kind, like how to run a capital campaign or how to choose a church school curriculum. Such topics really merit some form of continuing education event like a consultation or a seminar. They do not really require that you know one another and have built a sense of community together. Even though ministers often love to trade technical information when they get together (in part because it makes them feel, I think, like they have mastered something), ultimately you should strive not to address technical problems but deeper ones (sometimes the "impossible" ones, as discussed in the previous chapter) like how to inspire generosity in the first place and how to educate Christians formed by postmodern culture. Another reason to avoid problem solving is that members' unique contributions, perspectives, and backgrounds get lost in a purely technical discussion. In a community of practice, the members always matter and are not interchangeable. This is because wisdom is embodied in actual individuals with tacit knowledge based on years of experience. You want to exploit rather than ignore what each can uniquely teach the rest.

Of course, practitioners always have how-to problems on their minds. They will inevitably bring them into the group. Someone in your cohort might arrive one week having just been asked by his church's moderator whether the church should mount a capital campaign and he doesn't have any experience with them. Another may have recently met with the Christian education committee and realized she knew very little about the differences among church school curricula. They feel pressured to provide leadership on such matters within their congregations, so they come to their group seeking new ideas. Aware that others have raised funds and developed thriving educational programs, they want to hear how it was done. I did not stay with my dissertation writing group, after all, merely because I was committed to becoming a better writer in general; I came because I had chapters that needed completing! We are, after all, to a large extent what we *do*. Doing, thinking, and being are ultimately inseparable, and therefore part of being an excellent minister is knowing how to carry out the practical and even technical aspects of ministry. Therefore, you will want to take time to address them; just don't let them dominate the agenda of your group.

The third pitfall is becoming too focused on immediate problems at the expense of long-term interests. Naturally folks will have these on their minds as well. Someone may arrive at the meeting having just heard that her organist is resigning. Another may have learned that his grant proposal was rejected. Problems and events come at us randomly, especially in the ministry, and having a peer group meeting on the calendar does not stop them from occurring. Because immediate concerns and joys affect the state of our ministries, not to mention our minds and spirits, it would be almost cruel not to build in some time for reflecting on them. That having been said, group members also honor each other by honoring the purpose that brought them together. It can be frustrating to belong to a group that fails, time after time, to get around to its stated purpose. It is also all too easy to forget that *you yourselves* are the ultimate purpose of the group, and so you need to try not to dwell on the immediate crises of the day.

In the case of a group that has been organized around a particular domain of inquiry, it will be important to turn to that eventually, especially for those members who like following a plan. If you remain always in reactive mode, you probably won't be able to engage each other around those issues that are not pressing but are intellectually and spiritually nourishing. After all, it is the rare pastor who will arrive at a meeting stressed out because she can't decide whether Augustine believes in free will or determinism. But if your group intended to study Augustinian theology and you spend endless time on immediate pastoral concerns, you will be cheating yourselves of the kind of theological reflection you wanted. Peer groups are about finding relief and support from a caring community, but they are also about growing the mind.

To balance the need for addressing both practical and immediate concerns along with long-term interests, most groups intentionally take a while at the beginning of each meeting for prayer and checking in. This time also serves to reconstitute yourselves as a group. You have all spent the intervening days since you last met somewhere else, concerned about other things and other people. The group and its purpose may have been the last thing on your mind for a while. You need to transition back into it. It helps to take a moment to unburden yourselves of the most immediate and pressing things on your heart and mind. This time can also be devoted to personal sharing: "My daughter announced this week that she hates church." "My partner was diagnosed last month with cancer, and we're waiting to hear what his treatment will be." I said in the previous chapter that one function of a group is to be a safe holding environment for the stresses and challenges that come with ministry. An environment like this cannot be taken for granted. A group needs to be intentional about creating it anew every time it meets by carving out enough time for what is going on with people personally and professionally.

Some days, it may be difficult to decide when to move from the check-in period to your planned activities, if you have them. If something significant has come up in the life or work of one of the members, it can seem insensitive to transition too quickly away from talking about it. When I was leading peer reflection groups in divinity school (Practicum), I sometimes decided to jettison the discussion slated for that day because the concerns that surfaced were too important. In fact, I found that the more trust a group developed, the more students wanted to share with each other and the less need they had for me to prepare a formal discussion topic anyway. When ministers learn to be sufficiently reflective about their work and sufficiently attentive to each other as colleagues, their day-to-day ministries can provide enough fodder for a good discussion. But when you are lucky enough to have this happen, it means that you have succeeded in making technical and immediate problems more than technical and immediate! You will have instinctively learned to avoid the pitfalls I have warned against. You will have learned to do reflection on practice in the midst of practice. You will have already become reflective practitioners.

Q: What can we do to build our group in its formation stage?

Community is built when people know and trust one another, and this will happen when you listen to each other's stories. As I will argue in the last chapter of this book, communities built on relationship are stronger than communities of strangers. Of course, that chapter is about ministry in the public realm, where the importance of nurturing relationship in community may not be immediately obvious. (It may not seem to matter whether people who have joined together around a social justice issue actually know one another.) You might think that, surely, in a small group of peers who have voluntarily elected to gather to talk about ministry, trust can be assumed and that deep relationships will develop automatically. I am not so sure. I believe that many factors—including competition, the long history of isolationism, and a proclivity to introversion—get in the way of clergy really coming to know each other well, even when they are in a peer group.

Building trust is not just a matter of choosing at the outset people who like each other or are already familiar with each other. Trust doesn't arise from friendly feelings but from a process of risking openness. People who don't really enjoy relationships of deep trust just trade tidbits of advice; those who do trust are willing to hold a mirror up to themselves in front of each other. Your group won't arrive at the trust it needs instantly but rather through incremental steps of sharing ever more significant information about yourselves. As Wenger et al. say, "The trust community members need is not simply the result of a decision to trust each other personally. It emerges from understanding each other."[2] Meaningful reflection on practice also ultimately depends on mutual trust. As I said in the last chapter, you are trying to bring tacit knowledge to the surface, and this requires spending enough time and hearing enough stories from each other to really get a sense of who you all are and how you think.

Attention to building a trust community is especially important as the group is forming. Trust does not follow a timetable, but familiarity with each other and knowledge of common experiences will hasten it. "At the heart of a community's incubation period is the development of this deep insight into each other's individual practice, each other's reactions and style of thinking, and a collective understanding of the practice as a whole."[3] Therefore, it is a good idea to take time when the group is still new to do some storytelling.

What do I mean by storytelling? In this context, I mean telling each other the stories of how you ended up in the ministry or, even more specifically, how you ended up in this peer group as someone who cares about excellent ministry. In public life, as I will discuss in the last chapter of this book, the point of telling your stories is to learn how the other people tick. You ask and answer such questions as, "Who are you? What do you want? Why do you do what you do? Why don't you spend more time on what you say is most important to you?"[4] A peer group asks and answers the same questions. You don't just recite the facts of your life, like where you were born, where you went to school, and so forth, but you instead give an autobiographical narrative or testimony that reveals something about how you came to develop into the person you are with the passions that you have. You tell how God has been working in your life to bring you to this place and make you who you are.

Two examples from my own experience teaching Practicum will help answer the question of how storytelling can function in a peer group. The examples also show, incidentally, how easy it can be to *overlook* the importance of storytelling to community building. In both cases the value of incorporating it into the classroom impressed itself upon me almost by accident.

One year I was teaching a section of Practicum where students were responsible for leading the class sessions. One day well into the academic year, the designated leader showed up not having prepared a case or an activity for class as was typically expected. What she decided to do instead was simply tell others the tale of how she had come to be enrolled at divinity school and to prepare for ministry in her denomination. Hers was a particularly interesting story, and she told it with candor and humor. We came to see how unlikely a candidate for ministry she might have seemed only a few years back and yet also how fitting it was that she was in divinity school now. We learned things about her denomination, and how its limited opportunities for women had affected her, that we had never known. Many of us who had privately viewed her as rather "green" now recognized in her a young woman with a fair amount of grit and determination. When she finished telling her story, she asked others if they would share theirs. The class session ended up being a remarkable one. Students finally learned the back stories on each other that made sense of all the issues they had been bringing to class all year. They better understood how their respective calls to ministry had arisen and why they persisted in some of the questions and struggles that they had. In addition, they simply bonded. For the rest of the year, the class had a different feel to it. The storytelling even made a difference in the way they learned from each other when they resumed analyzing cases.

Another year, I was seeking to redesign Practicum in order to build more social analysis into it. I wanted students to see that their own stories of faith and call to ministry were situated within the larger context of religious and political history. I reasoned that we become the people we are in large part due to the personalities we were born with, the parents who raised us, and the psychological events that shaped us, but many of us tell our stories as though these private and personal factors are the only sorts of influences on us. We forget that we (and our ministries) are also deeply formed by the times in which we live and the social and political events that have occurred during them. Sometimes we need to be prompted to trace these influences, so individualistic is the typical American mindset regarding how we develop as people and professionals. So I created an assignment called the "Faith Time Lines Exercise." Students were to create a double time line of their lives, one line representing their own personal narrative (the year of their birth, significant events, time spent in and away from church, any conversion experiences, career changes, and so forth) and one line representing historical events and periods (for example, the political assassinations of the sixties, the fall of the Berlin Wall, the founding of their denomination, the attacks of 9/11, and the like). Then they would tell each other their life stories, using the parallel time lines as a way to situate their lives within a broader social context.

The semester of Practicum already had an ambitious agenda, full of cases about ministry that I thought were important to discuss. So I asked the teachers of the Practicum groups to devote one class session to the Faith Time Lines Exercise. Almost immediately, they reported back to me that one class session was not nearly enough. At our first teachers' meeting, held three weeks into the semester, some of them confessed that their groups hadn't yet gotten to the assigned cases, because they still hadn't completed the exercise. Students had too much to tell each other. Their lives were too interesting! What I had imagined as an exercise in social analysis, they were using as a way to build relationship. For example, the older students realized how different it must have been to come of age when the sixties and seventies (and even eighties) had already become "retro." The international students' stories made the Americans confront their parochialism. All of the students that year taught me that autobiographical storytelling is a powerful way to start a course. In subsequent years, we allowed several weeks for students simply to learn the stories of their fellow classmates before moving on to case studies.

In *Know Your Story and Lead with It*, Richard L. Hester and Kelli Walker-Jones relate their project of leading peer groups for twenty pastors over six years' time. These groups were explicitly built around telling the stories of their lives. The authors suggest beginning a group with a statement of purpose, such as "The purpose of this group is to give us ministers a place to tell our story, the narrative that is our life, to explore how our story equips us to be narrative leaders, and to create a safe community where we can say whatever is on our minds and hearts."[5] They contend that clergy have relatively few venues for unedited storytelling: ministers experience too much pressure to sound a certain way within their congregations, too much competition and too little safety in denominational contexts, and too much concern over being pigeonholed as a liberal or conservative. Groups provide "a place to examine the whole of

their story, their story unedited."[6] Even so, clergy actually have
to *learn* how to tell the stories of their lives. Hester and Walker-
Jones offer several techniques, including the recollection of ear-
liest childhood memories, drawing family trees, interviewing
each other, and crafting poems.[7]

You might be thinking that for some ministers, autobiographical storytelling is not a novel thing, that it doesn't really
take so long, and that not everyone needs to learn how to do
it. Clergy who have been shaped in an evangelical tradition, in
particular, are often familiar with the form of storytelling they
know as testimony. These ministers can often tell the stories
of their lives in a way that has been well honed over the years.
Indeed, testimony for them hasn't even been limited to church
settings. As theologian Philip Clayton writes:

> There is a long and rich tradition of "telling one's story" within
> most Christian denominations, including most of the main-
> line traditions. In the conservative evangelical world that first
> formed me as a Christian, we were asked to give our testimony
> so often that it became a highly formed and nuanced narra-
> tive, adaptable to multiple audiences. As a summer mission-
> ary in Europe during college, I learned to give my testimony
> in halting German to small groups of Austrian teenagers who
> had come to play soccer with us on their local soccer field.
> . . . As a member of the traveling brass choir at Westmont
> College, I would give my testimony to audiences during the
> programs we played at various churches. As a youth minister,
> I learned to adapt the narrative in ways that would inspire
> the youth to think about their own relationship with Jesus, so
> that they could learn to tell their own stories.[8]

Therefore evangelicals may have an initial advantage when it
comes to getting to know one another through storytelling. But
even while Clayton is attempting to say that it comes naturally
to all Christians ("Telling our own stories is just what we do

as human beings"),[9] I would argue that his examples describe a kind of narrative that has been subject to a fair amount of editing. As he says, his story was made to fit his audience. What clergy of all stripes may need to learn, then, is how to just talk candidly and not tell such polished stories of themselves. Or, if this is impossible given the biases and slants we all tend to lend our own narratives, then to listen to each other's stories with an ear to what might have been left out, embellished, or otherwise edited during the polishing process. In this way the group can come to know one another as a community of authentic selves.

Striving for authenticity right from the start is important. Even though I suggest storytelling as a strategy for getting to know one another and building trust, I do not mean to imply that you should just sit back and listen politely to your respective stories. Even when the group is new, it can begin learning how to insist on honesty, to probe for deeper meaning, and to unearth tacit knowledge. What you are after in a community of practice is to get beyond the superficial conversational practices we are all so adept at. The difficulty of getting there is, in my experience, not to be underestimated. Unless they are in an intentional setting like spiritual direction or a clinical pastoral education group, pastors do not tend to press each other to explain themselves. They tend to listen politely and sympathetically. They take what the other says at face value. Your group can change this. What Ed Chambers says about relational meetings in public life could just as well describe your aim for meetings of a peer group:

> The relational meeting isn't chitchat, like the usual informal exchange over coffee or drinks. In casual meetings, we take people as they present themselves. We don't push. We don't dig. We don't ask why or where a notion came from. We don't probe an idea. We don't raise possibilities. We don't ask questions that engage the imagination: "Well, what if you looked at it this way?" "How would your parents have reacted?"

"How would you feel if you were the other person?" In every-day, casual talk, we don't show depth of curiosity or interest, and we don't expect curiosity and interest to be demonstrated toward us.[10]

In a group that seeks to be a genuine community, you *will* do all these things.

Q: What can we do to learn from each other as our group progresses?

As your group takes shape, you will want to examine the min-istry practices around which you are gathered. You will become intentional about learning from each other through the shar-ing of your experiences in ministry. You will start asking each other the kinds of questions Chambers cites that "engage the imagination." One of the most time-honored ways of doing experience-based learning is the case study.

What is a case study? In essence, it is a way to bring oth-ers into a situation that they cannot themselves experience directly. I have frequently said that it helps to think of study-ing a case as a substitute for firsthand exposure. If your peers could show up at your place of ministry and become flies on the wall to watch events as they happen, that might be ideal, and we would have no need to write cases. But since the members of your group will likely be unavailable as spectators, you can use cases as a handy focus for reflection instead. A case may be defined as *a closely narrated description of an actual situation that is sufficiently interesting or thought provoking so as to invite differing interpretations.* A person bringing a case to a group for study does so because something is going on with her that merits group reflection and discussion. It sheds light on many aspects of her practice and hopefully theirs as well. To give an example, perhaps a pastor had been asked by a parishioner to keep a confidence and kept it, but then the secret leaked out anyway, and other members of the congregation got mad at the pastor for agreeing to the secrecy. The pastor now regrets how things turned out and feels partly culpable but also still feels she had good reasons for keeping the information secret. She wonders what her peers think. This situation goes not only to her ethics but also to her authority as a member of the clergy, her beliefs about community, and her theology of ministry. She writes the situation up in the form of a case, giving a little bit of background detail on the parishioner in question, telling how events unfolded, and describing where things stand now. She doesn't try to outline too many thoughts or feelings about what happened but rather tries to put the situation on paper with enough objectivity that her peers will be able to enter into it vicariously.

Cases are usually written, but they may simply be told to the group. When I have assigned written cases, I usually suggest they be about a page in length—that is, more than just brief summaries but less than full analyses of events. A case can describe a situation that is still unfolding or one that is past. Cases tend to be fairly detailed: they provide the information others need to understand the situation. At the same time, they are not mere "verbatims" or recitations of what happened when. They are more like stories. Some details will necessarily be left to the imagination of the readers. Cases are shaped by the writer or teller and inevitably reflect a point of view. Missiologist and proponent of case teaching Alan Neely defines one: "In essence, a case is a written description of an authentic event that is fraught with ambiguity. It is written from one person's perspective, seen through one person's eyes. All the information one might desire is not provided, because no one knows everything that happened or what everyone thought."[11] One might assume that cases are written by people facing knotty problems or dilemmas about which they must make crucial decisions. Sometimes this is why people bring forth cases, but not always. Cases don't always have to end with the question "What should I do now?" Neely's emphasis on *ambiguity* is salient. People bring cases to their peers for study because a situation they face has given them pause and caused them to speculate—on the meaning of ministry, on their theological views, on how the Spirit is moving in their life, and so on. Since it is essentially a slice of real life, a case contains all the nuance that real life does. It is not just a problem to be solved. Other people can help the one bringing the case reflect not only on future courses of action but also on how the situation might have arisen in the first place, when it was that events took a significant turn, and why the different characters acted the way they did. Others might share times they faced similar incidents or help analyze the conditions operating in the situation that make it unlike anything they have ever experienced. Their knowledge about ministry is brought in to "scaffold" the case bringer's own knowledge, as discussed in the previous chapter.

From the case bringer's perspective, using cases in peer groups has many benefits. On the one hand, other people can usually see things about an experience that he hasn't noticed. When Neely said that "no one knows everything that happened or what everyone thought," that includes the case bringer. He can get so wrapped up in the situation he is going through that he fails to see aspects of it. Let's say he has related a story about a contentious church council meeting where a proposal of his was shot down. He interprets his story as one of his pastoral authority being undermined. A member of his group, on the other hand, might be able to see it from the council's point of view. They might ask him, "Do you think perhaps council members reacted that way to your proposal because they had tried something similar years before and it hadn't worked? Many of them have, after all, been members of your church since long before you became pastor." His group can even challenge him to lose his blind spots. On the other hand, peers can also provide corrective when a case bringer might be reading things into situations that are *not* there. For example, someone might have brought a case about an interaction with a parishioner she found particularly difficult. She assumes one of the problems is that the parishioner doesn't respect her because of her youthful age, but someone in her group can say, "Isn't that the guy you've told us about who is always blunt when speaking his mind? Perhaps he complained about the hymns you chose because he just didn't like them! Maybe it isn't about lack of respect at all."

Of course, *anybody* might be able to provide additional eyes and ears on a situation when told about it. The advantage to using cases with *peers* is that they know each other well, know how each thinks and how each is wired. Because they are peers, they also know more than many people will about what it's like to be in a particular position. All of us are always in the process of making meaning(s) of our experience. We do this in part by constructing an event we have experienced as an event *of* something. What I see as a case of misconduct you might see as a case of a dysfunctional family system. We each interpret cases according to where we stand relative to them. We bring our own ministerial minds to bear upon them, and those minds have been shaped in different ways. Your peers know how *your* mind works and why.

Recently I had an interesting e-mail exchange with a colleague after we had both read the same blog describing a case about confidentiality. He was disturbed because the case writer didn't seem to take the pastoral needs of the confider into account. I hadn't shared that sense of disturbance at all. I had read the case from my perspective as an ethicist and took it to be a case of flawed ministerial judgment about a secret's impact on a community. He had read it from his perspective as a local church pastor as a case of inadequate pastoral care when listening to a secret. (He had, incidentally, once been told a confidence very similar to the one described, a position I have never directly been in.) At the end of our e-mail exchange, we both agreed that we had enjoyed having each other as conversation partners. Because we had known each other awhile, we knew that we could count on getting the ethicist's and the pastor's view from each other. Our exchanges are an example of the experience of "going meta" that I talked about in the previous chapter. We share not only our perspectives on ministry but also how we come by those perspectives.

The method of using cases is designed to prompt reflection on our practice and on ourselves as practitioners. Even in the initial act of composition, cases allow their authors to be self-reflective. A case, after all, is just a slightly more formal vehicle than an off-the-cuff rendition of what someone has experienced. But the formality has its advantages. There is nothing like having to find the words to describe an experience to discover what meaning the experience holds. The discipline of composing a case gives us distance. It works like the old ruse of going to someone for advice by saying, "I have this friend who . . ." when it is really us with the problem. In the process of writing about ourselves, even if we write in the first person, we become like characters in a story. We become simultaneously both object and subject of our experience. Hear how one seminary student described the case writing process: "As I prepared the case for the group, based on a life situation I was personally struggling with, I was given the opportunity to achieve a greater degree of objectivity than I had prior to the act of writing. Once put on paper, the case had a life beyond my original personal perspective." The same student goes on to describe what it was like to have her case discussed by her class: "My individual manner of dealing with various life possibilities was held up in a mirror before my face. . . . Through the responses and caring of each group member during class discussion of my case, and after prayer and further reflection, I acted on the composite insights of the group."[12]

Once you have brought a case to your peers, it then helps you, as this example shows, by giving you a chance to receive their insights and reflections. Most teachers and facilitators who use a case study method require the author to stay silent while the case is being discussed. Once you have brought the case and answered any factual questions about it that the group finds necessary in order to discuss it, you just listen. You cannot rebut or argue with someone's reflection by saying, "No, that's not right, because . . ." Sometimes you may find that the discussion goes off in a direction that is not necessarily implied by the details of the case. (This is what the student quoted on the previous page may have meant by a case taking on a life of its own.) You might feel tempted to jump in and redirect your peers back to what you know to be the facts and what you think to be the salient points. But it's best if you do not, for several reasons. First, this is the time when the group assumes ownership of your case. Ministry becomes the community property I talked about in the previous chapter. The situation is no longer just yours but, in a sense, theirs as well. You benefit from this because it makes you feel less isolated. Second, even when a group appears to be taking liberty with what really happened, the results of their musings can be revealing. At the very least, you get a chance to reflect privately on why you think an idea from the group is off target. Thinking to yourself, "Maya wouldn't have believed something like that" might make you realize that theology matters to the case in a way you had not adequately conveyed when writing it and perhaps didn't even fully appreciate. Third, listening gives you the space to consider and accept what the group says about your situation. If you don't have to talk, you can probably take their reflections more seriously.

The important thing is not to use cases simply as a means of getting your group's vote on what you ought to do. Even though the student quoted on the previous page speaks of acting on the composite insights of her group, the point is not necessarily to figure out what immediate steps to take next. In my experience, a group discussing a case nearly always wants to go there first. They want to tell you what to do, not only because technical solutions are always tempting but also simply because they have compassion for you. However, groups that rush to fix the problems by suggesting courses of action nearly always miss important aspects of the case and opportunities to dig more deeply. What your group is also there for is to be careful interpreters, to help you discern what is important and unimportant about the situation, to think theologically with you about your role in it, to play devil's advocate if need be, to challenge you with probing questions, and to pray with you. Sometimes simple silence works wonders. As a facilitator, I almost always use some method of theological reflection (role playing, imagination, even forms of artistic and dramatic response) just to move groups away from the problem-solving stance they will otherwise try to take. Even if they are allowed to give concrete advice after a time of reflection, the advice will have been grounded in theological insights they might not have discovered otherwise. Perhaps one of the most important functions of the group, in addition, is to serve as a collective memory. Your cohorts can follow up with you later, see how things went, and refer back to your case weeks later when its particulars may have faded but its lessons still resonate.

Treating cases as technical problems also has a way of letting everybody feel like situations in ministry are resolvable with enough foresight and smart thinking. "If you had only done x, then this case wouldn't have arisen" is a common and tempting response. Tempting because we want to think that nothing like that would ever happen to us. But not only do we sometimes inherit problems in the church, we also sometimes make mistakes ourselves! Taking the time to consider our own and others' mistakes is well worth it, because these messes are frequently the kind we find ourselves mired in. In addition, as I affirmed in the previous chapter, sometimes ministry is just downright hard, so there are many problems you will encounter that in the end admit of no simple solutions. I have heard many case discussions end with the group saying something to the effect of, "Well, there's just no easy answer here. Good luck to you," only to watch the case bringer express not dismay, strangely enough, but relief. It can be a solace to know that your peers couldn't have done any better than you, that what you find daunting is universally daunting, that there are many possible ways to go forward, and that, in the end, what happens in ministry isn't all about you anyway.

One final word about methodology: Cases are most effective when discussed in the context of a fairly structured conversation. This is because they represent actual situations that arise from and affect someone's ministry and can therefore make case bringers feel vulnerable when bringing them forward. In their peer group methodology, Hester and Walker-Jones follow a case presentation schedule that divides the hour into precise segments: the author presents the case to a partner for twenty minutes, followed by one minute of silence, fourteen minutes of group reflection, ten minutes of author response, and fifteen minutes of open discussion.[13] In the Practicum groups that I ran, we simply had the author read the case aloud, remain silent for the discussion, and then take about five minutes at the end to respond. If such a structure for case studies sounds excessively formal and off-putting to you, I would remind you that structure actually keeps discussions safe and constructive. As Hester and Walker-Jones put it, "To present a problem to a group without clear structures can be an intimidating and unnerving experience. The presenter doesn't know what's going to happen next; and there's too much opportunity for intrusive, critical, judgmental, not curious, or otherwise inappropriate questions."[14] Your group members might offer inappropriate responses regardless of what method you follow, but at least following some sort of schedule helps contain them to a specific period of time. One of the most powerful experiences I ever had bringing a case to a group was at a conference for women who all occupied similar professional positions. The point of the gathering was to provide career direction and support for those of us in these positions. We were to bring a one-page description of our current work. When the small group I was assigned to worked on my case, I was able to see my job and its challenges through their eyes. The experience was stimulating and thought provoking but also made me somewhat self-conscious. I recall being tired when my turn was over and glad for the time constraints. Some members of your group may relish being in the spotlight forever, but for those who don't, following a consistent schedule will be a blessing.

Checking in, storytelling, and case-based learning are three ways to structure the time a clergy peer group spends together. There are many other activities you could jointly engage in to become better ministers. Do not forget to pray together. I have not written about prayer, because it is not so much a separate activity as an undergirding to anything you do together. But you will want to hold one another not only before each other but also before God.

Q: Do peer groups need facilitators?

Not all groups necessarily need someone to facilitate their time together, but experience shows that groups that have facilitators are different from groups that don't. By a facilitator, I mean *someone who has had at least some training in group process and listening skills and who is set aside from the rest of the group for leading discussion, if not necessarily the entire group experience.* (That is, the facilitator may or may not be the one also sending out meeting reminders, arranging lunch, and so forth.) Some peer groups compensate their facilitators while in others it is a voluntary role.

You have probably gathered from some of the foregoing descriptions of doing check-in, using case studies, and telling stories that facilitators can make a difference. At the very least they can keep time and keep people on task. They can guide the transitions from one part of the meeting to the next. They can help steer group members away from the very common tendency to start feeding each other advice and fixing each other's problems. They can facilitate good listening. Many of us have been trained in listening skills such as offering nonjudgmental feedback, watching for body language, and so on, but even the best of us readily forget how to listen well when we encounter a colleague who seems to need our input. Facilitators can effectively be the people who foster the trust that is so crucial to developing good groups.

Some of these same functions can, of course, be carried out by the group collectively. The two communities of practice of my own that I described in the previous chapter lacked facilitators. Our graduate school potluck dinners certainly constituted a very meaningful experience of community in my life, even though no one facilitated them. Conversation simply flowed at leisure. However, as I also pointed out when I was describing that group, we had other venues for accomplishing more formal tasks such as responding to each other's work, and those other venues were facilitated. In my dissertation writing group, we organized ourselves according to a pattern. When it was your turn to bring a piece of your writing for critique, you told the rest of the group what kind of feedback you were seeking and what aspects of the draft you hoped they would pay most attention to, and then you got to sit back, take notes, and absorb what they said. Generally I recall that somebody else kept track of time and moved things along. When you were a reader, you shared responsibility for making sure that the conversation was helpful to the writer. The division of responsibility tended to work, I think, because we had a rather specific agenda and a "product" in front of us motivating us to keep each other on task.

Perhaps you have had experience with groups where no one is designated the facilitator or where facilitation is rotated among the members. The advantages are the sense of informality and spontaneity that result and the freedom to collectively decide to do whatever you want to do. The main disadvantages of nonfacilitated groups tend to be the unpredictability of shared leadership and lack of a center. A group can usually carry on pretty well for a while without someone at the center, especially ones that gather around a discrete task (such as critiquing drafts of written work), if they already know and trust one another, and if they are equally well equipped at whatever task they are undertaking. But if they do not necessarily know each other and are brought together with the somewhat nebulous goal of supporting each other's development in ministry, they may need a facilitator's help to create the atmosphere in which that goal can be met.

Twenty years ago congregational consultant, educator, and author Roy Oswald made a case for paid leadership of clergy peer groups in his book *Clergy Self-Care*. His argument was that a leader enables trust to develop because everyone knows they can rely on him or her to pay attention to group process and therefore the rest can be freed to just express their needs and feelings. "It's a gift to be able to come panting into a trusted group of peers and have someone take charge and say, 'Let's spend a few minutes in silence to get ourselves totally here, and then let's each take five minutes to share the highs and lows of our week.'"[15] Oswald argued that clergy so often depend on resources within themselves that they sometimes need to be invited to enter a state of "extra-dependence." This is a state "in which I am dependent upon a resource outside of me that I feel is trusting and caring therefore allowing me to play, experience my essence, experience Grace or Sabbath time, or to just BE."[16] My adult sisters and I often used to indulge in a version of extra-dependence when we traveled back to our family home on vacation. We would spend the first day or so of our time there in our old bedrooms taking long naps. Our mother always put up a mock protest—"Everybody just sleeps when they come home!"—but she would say it with a smile. She un-

derstood that home is the place where adults can be children
again. She knew that on some level she was entrusted to be in
charge and to take care of things while the rest of the family
relaxed, and she accepted (and even relished) that role. Clergy
are like weary adult children. It is precisely because they lack
sufficient opportunity to enter into an extra-dependent state
in their workaday lives that clergy need peer groups. Oswald
was saying that groups with facilitators let them enter this state
even more quickly. "No one moves easily to a state of Extra-dependence until they perceive strength and caring at the center
of the experience."[17]

I think Oswald was correct. In any event, since his time,
enough research has been done on clergy peer groups to support at least the general observation that facilitation makes a
difference to a group, if not his specific theory about the need
for facilitators. Sociologist of religion Penny Long Marler has
shown that self-directed groups (those without trained facilitators) are correlated with the following features: they are smaller, more homogeneous groups of people who find each other
through already established networks and who do not desire a
highly structured experience but rather are looking for a regular opportunity for fellowship with other clergy. Members of
these groups may have other avenues for continuing education
but nevertheless seek relief from the stress of their work. She
has found that groups with trained facilitators, in contrast,
tend to draw a more diverse membership of people who did not
necessarily know each other before, who seek an opportunity
for learning and enrichment in an atmosphere of structure and
accountability.[18] Therefore it seems safe to say that the decision
to hire a facilitator would depend on the kind of group you are
seeking to form. At the same time, evidence suggests that trust
can flourish in both facilitated and self-directed groups, even
if it may take longer in the latter, and both kinds of groups
can develop into healthy and productive ones where significant
learning takes place. As some directors of peer group programs

point out, clergy do not always have the luxury of gatherings that are facilitated; perhaps they would do well to learn how to learn from their peers even when no one is shepherding them.[19]

Q: How much should a peer group cost?

The question of hiring a paid facilitator is closely related to the question of cost; obviously, paying a stipend will increase the cost to the group. Facilitators should ideally belong to a community of practice of their own so that they receive support for and continuing training in the work they are doing with you. This would add to the total time they devote to their role, and hence to their compensation. Other expenses associated with running a peer group program might include meals, lodging, travel reimbursement, books and other materials, and honoraria for any guest speakers or trainers. In practice, clergy peer groups run the gamut from those with quite modest budgets to those with large ones. Expense depends on the nature of the group and its aims.

One feature that appears to hold constant in the success of peer groups, however, is the importance of hospitality. It is worth including some hospitality expenses in your budget. As Oswald noted, as clergy you are like anybody else in needing a place to go to be taken care of for a while. Spending money to have meals provided at the location where your group meets, for example, may seem like a small detail, but it goes a long way. When you are freed even from the small task of bringing a sack lunch for yourself, you can enter more fully into the experience of being a group member who only has to pay attention to the group. The same logic applies to other hospitality-related expenses—say, for overnight accommodations if the group travels together or meets at a distant location. The more effort members have to give to arranging their own comfort, the more distracted they will tend to be. This does not mean you have to stay at four-star hotels when you go on retreat (which might introduce other kinds of distractions!), but giving some advanced attention to the arrangements will generally make the meeting go more smoothly.

In addition, hospitality makes the difference between an experience about which people might still feel unsure and one they feel honored to be part of. For several years I ran a summer program for divinity students that began with two weeks of intensive, all-day training in leadership skills. I insisted that lunch be part of the day, and generally I took the whole group out to eat together in a restaurant. Usually the first couple of times we went out, students would hesitate when ordering and ask whether lunch was really complimentary, but slowly they relaxed into the luxury of a nice meal. I let them order whatever they wanted (within reason); as a leader with a sweet tooth, I frequently invited the group to indulge in dessert! Every year as I presented the program budget to the dean, I had to defend the cost of those lunches. Prudence might have dictated, after all, that we break at midday and let students be responsible for their own meals. But I believed that eating together was highly valued and highly valuable. Not only did the lunches let the class bond and allow for conversation to continue in a more informal manner—the arguments for the importance of fellowship—but they also simply let the students luxuriate and feel special, which is often a rare feeling for students qua students. I felt providing lunch sent a message that their participation was valued and that how they were being formed over the summer was important not only to them but also to the school.

To emphasize the importance of hospitality is not necessarily to argue, however, that peer group members should never *contribute* to hospitality and other program costs. Making a financial contribution to an endeavor, after all, often increases one's commitment to it. Indeed, evidence suggests that there is a correlation between contributing to the cost of a peer group and experiencing a greater impact from it.[20]

Q: Should we aim for a homogeneous or diverse group?

Ministers' legitimate need for safety and support sometimes overshadows other goals, especially the importance of learning across lines of difference. Imagine a clergyperson who has been in many groups before and brings a laundry list of requirements for one you are creating. She tells you, "Well, I think it should be a gathering for smart, liberal, creative types who have hit a midcareer point and who are dedicated to supporting each other in revitalizing their ministries. That's the kind of group I would attend. I don't want to have to deal with neophytes or conservatives. We should all bring significant parish experience and a commitment to progressive politics in the church and world. Also, I'd insist on vegan meals and I wouldn't want to have to drive too far." My point is that some of us think that forming a group of people *like ourselves* will provide the optimal experience. The assumption is understandable. Especially for those who have in the past suffered through experiences of being the only one who was different, it can bring great relief finally to talk about ministry with others who automatically get it. They don't have to spend a lot of time explaining (or worse, defending) what it's like to be, say, female or gay or Pentecostal as a pastor. As I look back on my own experience with my writing group, for example, I realize it might have been easier in one way to invite only other students from the religious studies department. For me there was always the subtle burden of being the only one who was practiced in thinking theologically. Since members of my group were from different disciplines, we all had to bring each other up to speed about our particular perspectives and styles of argumentation.

And yet, the overwhelming evidence suggests that peer groups that embody diversity are ultimately more successful than homogeneous ones. It might seem both more practical and more comfortable to form groups along lines of denomination, theological persuasion, and other identity features. It might also seem quicker that way to arrive at the trust needed for those who "come panting" into them, as Oswald put it. But in the end, it appears that most people find the challenge of conversing with those different from them more stimulating than onerous. In fact, some clergy peer groups work hard at diversifying themselves, because they know they do not want to just be a bunch of people who look and talk and think the same. Particular attention has been paid to the value of crossing denominational lines. In fact, in his study of clergy clusters as a model for continuing education, Tim Dolan claims, "The single most significant factor in creating a safe space to share was the interdenominational makeup of the clusters. All cluster participants indicated that the interdenominational makeup made the clusters safe and easier for them to share at a deep level."[21] My own experience at an interdenominational divinity school confirms his observation. You might think that students attending such a school would want to be assigned to a peer reflection group made up of their denominational peers, but in ten years I never received this request. In fact I often heard the opposite: "Don't put me in a Practicum group with a bunch of others just like me," they would say. While students didn't necessarily want to be the only one of their type, they didn't want to be surrounded by their type.

The benefits of diversity are, first, that you learn to articulate better the language and concepts you take for granted. The Lutheran has to explain why he talks about grace so often. The Baptist confesses that she doesn't understand all the fuss others make around celebrating weekly Eucharist. Second, you learn a great deal from others whose background and perspective you might never otherwise be exposed to. Even the occasional conflict that arises from difference can be salutary if it is sufficiently resolved. Clergy can bring the experience of clashing with a colleague, and yet surviving, into their conflict-prone ministries. Finally, there is nothing like bonding with a group of people very different from yourself to prove the value of small community. We have precious few experiences, sometimes, of learning to lean personally and professionally on "unlikely suspects," and therefore we treasure all the more those occasions of trusting and being entrusted by people we never would have sought out on our own. I dare even say that peer groups built on diversity teach us something of the meaning of being church.

The one kind of homogeneity recommended by those who study clergy peer groups is putting clergy together according to their tenure in the ministry. There are so many issues unique to being new to the ministry, and others that only seasoned clergy share, that mixing new and seasoned clergy can be less effective. The latter don't want to have to serve as mentors to their younger colleagues when they are in a group whose purpose is to develop themselves. At the same time, new clergy don't relish the burden of representing the "cutting edge" of the profession to their senior colleagues or, alternatively, risking the appearance of naiveté. I might argue that a good facilitator should be able to prevent members from slipping into these roles, and that we need more rather than fewer discussions across generational lines if the church is going to survive into the future, but I acknowledge that other venues may be more appropriate than peer groups.

Q: What rules of confidentiality should we follow?

The importance of mutual trust to the success of a peer group cannot be overemphasized. To engage in serious and intentional reflection on your practice and on yourself as a practitioner, you will have to become vulnerable. To become vulnerable, you will have to trust the members of your group. Eventually you will want to reach a level of sharing that goes beyond mere reporting to the ways your ministry is challenging you. You won't reach this level if an atmosphere of competition or posturing reigns. You won't reach it if sharing gets reduced to whining. As I said in the previous chapter, ministry is genuinely difficult and people sometimes expect ministers to be flawless human beings. For these reasons you need a place where you can be candid about the difficulty without worrying about how you come across. Certainly you need the assurance that your doubts and insecurities will not be broadcast outside of the group. To make your groups safe and productive places for mutual sharing, then, you should generally agree not to repeat outside of the group what you learned about each other inside the group.

Depending on the ethos of your denomination or region, where gatherings of colleagues may or may not be considered confidential spaces, a rule of confidentiality in your peer group may be quite countercultural and take some getting used to. Sometimes we have to remind ourselves where it was we learned a particular piece of information—say, about the impending resignation of a colleague—and train ourselves not to repeat it if we learned it in our group.

Let me add a word about confidentiality with regard to the use of cases. You might hesitate to bring a case, not because it makes you feel vulnerable but because it reflects badly on characters whose behavior you tell about. If you are going to bring real rather than hypothetical cases, you will effectively be sharing information about people in your church "behind their back." You should therefore change names and disguise identifying details in your cases. Group members should not keep copies of written cases once the discussion is over. More important, you should choose only to relate situations that shed significant light on your ministry, not just dramatic or sensational ones that will impress your peers and make for juicy discussion. Ultimately your goal is to respect the people in your church by learning from your ministry among them.

Confidentiality, however, is not the same thing as privacy. Peer groups are not private clubs or cliques. Members don't keep insights and ideas to themselves if what is learned would benefit their congregations. The point is to produce knowledge about the practice of ministry, not hoard it. So wisdom, if not personal information, should be shared beyond the group and even capitalized upon. Ultimately, clergy peer groups should transform the wider church and not only individual ministers who belong to them.

Q: Should you tell your congregation that you belong to a peer group?

I have emphasized throughout my discussion that peer groups create safe spaces for clergy to retreat to. You might have concluded that it is unimportant or even unwise to tell your congregation that you belong to one. Why must they know that you meet monthly with your colleagues to talk about how your ministry is going? Might they not get suspicious of your need for outside support? Will they worry that you are not strong enough to handle the work? Or, perhaps more likely, will they start to resent the time that membership in a group takes away from your work? Sometimes clergy have been known to forego participation in continuing education events because they don't want to have to justify to their congregations the time and expense involved.

I understand the reasons for hesitancy. However, by giving in to them, clergy only reinforce the very conditions that need to change within the profession of ministry. For too long, congregations have intentionally or unintentionally perpetuated the myth of the self-sufficient, all-capable pastor who needs no support. They need to learn that pastors are real people who experience professional isolation and job pressure and who therefore deserve time with colleagues who are facing the same challenges. Congregations must also somehow come to better appreciate the need for clergy continuing education and value the time their pastors spend improving their skills and enriching their knowledge. While the burden of educating congregations should not rest on clergy alone, keeping a secret of your participation in a peer group won't help. Perhaps talking about peer groups as a community of practice will help, as some members of your congregation might be able to identify with or at least appreciate this concept. Sharing wisdom you have gained will also benefit them.

Q: How do peer groups come to a close?

Since a clergy peer group is an organic community, you shouldn't expect that it will live forever. We often grieve the loss of regular gatherings when they come to an end, especially if they have been meaningful and helpful to us, but endings must occur eventually. Sometimes a group ends simply because too many of its members move away or their interests change. Sometimes the funding dries up or the sponsoring organization (seminary, denomination) cannot support the program any longer and other resources cannot be found. Frequently members of self-defined groups without an established curriculum from a sponsor have trouble continuing to define their own purpose. What started out as a learning community increasingly turns into a social club, or the group simply loses its original momentum. Of course, sometimes a group ends for disappointing reasons, such as an irresolvable conflict, too many tensions among the membership, or bad leadership.[22]

Experience also shows, however, that members of some groups continue to meet even after the formal program ends. Whether or not your group follows this path will probably depend on your willingness to foot the cost yourselves or find another source of funding, and whether you can facilitate yourselves. Making the transition from a facilitated group into one that meets on its own can be difficult, for all the reasons given previously in this chapter. There is no shame in admitting that you relied on the structures provided by the program; they were put in place for a reason. Alternatively, your group may discontinue its original incarnation but take on a new life. In particular, many former peer group members find that the individual relationships they formed last beyond the group and function in many of the same ways for them as the whole group once did. Some also go on to form new communities of practice in new settings, having had a sufficiently good experience that they want to replicate it.

GETTING TOGETHER WITH YOUR PEERS to talk about ministry may seem like an ordinary practice in the pursuit of excellence. My hope is that this chapter, along with the previous one, has convinced you that your peers constitute a simple but profound resource for you. Treat your ministry as the valuable community property that it is, to be shared with others who love it.

5

Prophet, Priest, or King? Developing as a Leader in Public Ministry

THIS BOOK IS ABOUT HOW ministers can contribute to their own formation for excellent ministry. To be *formed* means letting yourself grow through commitment to new practices. So far the chapters have outlined processes or habits useful to any realm within ministry. This chapter is different in that it focuses on formation specifically for leadership in public ministry. There is no one right way to develop as a leader in public ministry, and you can probably become an adequate if not effective leader in part by happenstance, but as with any area within ministry, intentionality about leadership will increase your chances of becoming excellent at it.

Let me begin by inviting you to consider the following scenario—a case in miniature—drawn from a minister's public life. Whether the particular situation is typical for you will depend on the ministry you are called to, but it presents the minister with a decision that is typical: Should I get involved, and if so, how?

The town where you pastor a church has seen a steady increase in recent years of immigrants from Mexico and other Central and South American countries. None have joined your church, but you see them each morning congregating in the grocery store parking lot waiting for work as day laborers, and you are colleagues with the Catholic priest whose church many of them attend. You know that some of these new immigrants have become citizens but that most of them are undocumented. Some people have been grumbling about this in town but no real controversy has yet erupted. Without much warning, then, early one morning officials from US Immigration and Customs Enforcement conduct a raid and arrest nineteen young men from the parking lot and take them away to an unknown location. Suddenly the religious community in your town begins to mobilize. Your Catholic colleague leaves you a phone message asking you to attend a meeting of a new coalition that has formed to respond to the raid and to the larger cause of a more just immigration policy.

Public ministry refers, most basically, to any ministry where clergy and laity become engaged in issues and problems that are larger than their own community of faith. Public ministry focuses on the concerns we all have in common. For many, this will mean the big societal challenges like homelessness, poverty, war, or immigration, but for others, as we shall see, common concerns will be defined more locally and might include such matters as traffic calming, city ordinances, and street crime. It is difficult to be a minister today and not be drawn into some form of involvement in public life. All but the most isolationist leaders recognize the need and the call to be active in their wider communities. As pastoral theologian Gaylord Noyce wrote back in 1988, "Both the biblical tradition and the idea of a profession mandate our 'public ministry.' This emerging term points to the aspects of our work that are often labeled 'prophetic,' but it addresses today's actual pastoral office more comprehensively. The term *public ministry* reminds us that the pastor is beholden to far larger claims than the wishes of a particular congregation. . . . The minister is called to see congregation-building and pastoral caring within a controlling social vision that involves doing justice and loving mercy in faithfulness to God."[1]

And yet, some define public ministry not as doing justice but as providing service and supporting charitable concerns—work that is often called outreach. Charity is vital to community, and people of faith are called to practice it. But I have justice in mind. Public ministers mobilize people's power to effect lasting change; they do not simply recruit others in order to meet needs. Our scenario on page 140, after all, does not merely get you involved in outreach. Instead, you are called upon to become aligned with a particular group's interest, to stand with them and take action with them. The group is seeking change away from the way things are and toward the way they think things should be. Change frequently creates tension—because surely other groups in town have competing interests that would move things in a different direction. Saul Alinsky, founder of the Industrial Areas Foundation, coined what he called the "law of change," which he explains as follows: "Change means movement; movement means friction; friction means heat; heat means controversy."[2] In fact, what may make our scenario difficult for many of you, I suspect, is the way it might implicate you in political tension of some kind. The situation is potentially divisive and controversial.

I am convinced that most clergy want to figure out how to exercise public leadership. Having worked with students as they are just embarking on their professional ministries, I know that many worry that public ministry might isolate or exhaust them, or that it may simply get them into too much trouble! And yet I have also heard scores of them express a deep and insistent passion for justice. They want to act on their passion so as not to lose it, and they only wish they knew how.

Prophet, Priest, or King?

I tell students that the question of how to be involved in public life is, in large part, a question of *role*. What role do you see yourself adopting? To that end it might be helpful to recall the long tradition of pastors making sense of the ministerial role by invoking the threefold nature of Jesus's own ministry. According to this tradition, his redemptive work in the world was accomplished in his ongoing ministry as prophet, priest, and king. Jesus's ministerial role has long served as a metaphor for the ministry of all believers, ordained and lay alike, in both Catholic and Protestant traditions. To minister in Jesus's name is to become, like him, a prophet, a priest, and a king. Of course we can never be Jesus—this is why it remains a metaphor—but we are called to fulfill these same roles in our own time and context.

I find the prophet-priest-king tradition helpful to a discussion of public ministry for two reasons. The first is that the tradition reminds us that all roles are valid. Jesus's ministerial identity could not be neatly summed up into one word, and neither can ours. As ministers we move between multiple identities and roles. We can be a prophet *and* a priest *and* a king all in the same person, even if we primarily identify with one image the most. Second, this tradition functions helpfully by reminding us of the kingly or regent role in particular. I have found that very often, the choice about how to be involved as a minister in public or political matters gets framed in an overly simple binary way: as a choice between being prophetic or being pastoral. It is as though you have only two choices, and mutually exclusive ones at that. The prophet-priest-king tradition helps because it presents a third way to be.

PROPHECY

Prophecy is the ministry of communicating. The prophets of old knew how to give voice to the demands of justice, especially by speaking out on behalf of the marginalized and forgotten. Modern-day prophets urge others, by deed and especially by word, to see things anew and think in new ways. Through their preaching and teaching and public witness, they get the rest of us to feel the weight of injustice. They open our minds by delivering powerful indictments of the way things are and proclaiming a vision for how things ought to be. The virtues of a prophet include the ability to articulate what others are missing. The image from the prophet Joel is often lifted up as a quintessential expression of prophetic ministry: "Your sons and your daughters shall prophesy, your old men shall dream dreams, and your young men see visions" (2:28). Prophetic ministry is about giving voice to dreams and visions. It requires both courage and imagination. Prophets accomplish their work in many ways: by telling stories, crafting poetic utterance, and testifying to the truth. They "speak truth to power."

In the scenario that opened the chapter, I can well imagine you taking on the prophetic role. You might reflect carefully on the matter at hand before reaching a decision, but you would eventually say something to your flock. You would summon the courage, even if you knew what you had to say was potentially controversial. You would speak out on the problems of immigration. You might do so by preaching from the pulpit on them. You might write an article for the newsletter or the newspaper. You might lead an adult forum or workshop on immigration reform. But you would use your position of authority to make some sort of proclamation about the vision you have for the way things should be. You would take your place in the long history of clergy who communicate the truth as they see it, come what may.

Clergy have adopted various styles of prophetic witness over the years. Perhaps still most resonant in the memory of many of us are the members of the clergy who rode buses and walked in marches and got arrested in large numbers during the civil rights movement in the United States. We remember them because they were courageous and unafraid to act on their conscience and speak out about what was happening in the country at the time. For a long time, they defined what it meant to do public ministry. As Noyce writes, "The 1960s saw a remarkable increase in public ministry. On the spur of the moment, local pastors packed their bags and left for Selma, or Washington, or Jackson, to participate in the Civil Rights movement. They meant to bring a witness of the church to the public order."[3]

We can all think of prophets in the ministry today. Imagine the pastor of a large Protestant urban church who identifies himself as a theologian at heart. He loves to engage people in his congregation on the theologies of justice. He leads them in adult forums and studies where he can tell them about the theological heritage running through their tradition that supports the church's social justice concerns. Above all, he loves preaching. He feels at home in the pulpit and truly finds a voice there. He preaches on political matters and doesn't necessarily mind the hot water he occasionally gets in for doing so. He is in fact reasonably successful in his attempts to proclaim his vision to his congregation and get them engaged in it. His fortitude and fiery words are admired and remembered by many. They are proud of him and the witness he makes before them to the causes of justice.

Another sort of prophet comes to mind as well. Imagine someone who is more of a prophet in her local community. She writes op-ed pieces for the newspaper on a regular basis and also frequently gets her name in other sections of the paper for her activism on a range of social issues but especially the environment. She is known as one of the clergy members who can be counted on to show up for actions on environmental justice. She organizes the local Earth Day celebration every year and has spearheaded campaigns to change legislation on clean energy policy. At every church gathering she urges participants to adopt practices that will reduce their carbon footprint.

There are many admirable things about prophetic ministry. Such pastors stand in a long tradition of clergy who have spoken out against injustice, even and especially when few others around would join in. The church would be the poorer if it lacked such members of the clergy willing to be a witness to the gospel this way. And yet at the same time, even while I do not wish to denigrate prophetic ministry, it is fair to ask whether a prophetic model is the best or only model for public ministry. Even Noyce raises implicit questions as he remembers how pastors of the 1960s justified their activism to their people (and sometimes to themselves): "Clergy in both the Civil Rights and the antiwar movements believed their actions were conscience-building for the community of faith. . . . Some clergy argued that their independent activism was superbly educational, for people were growing as they came to terms with their pastor's actions, ex post facto. Others, more cautious, tried for congregational discussion in advance, or even carefully explained that their activism was on their free time, their days off."[4]

Noyce's recollection of the various justifications clergy gave for their public witnessing during the 1960s give us insight for today. Key, I think, is the word *independent* that he uses. The main problem with a prophetic style of ministry is that it is too often exercised independently of the congregation. The stereotypical image of the prophet, after all, is of a voice speaking in the wilderness. As a model of leadership, prophecy does not necessarily gather the community around to talk to one another. It does not always remember to seek the will of the listeners; sometimes prophets do not even know their audiences very well. Prophecy does not necessarily consult or cajole or organize. Indeed, it is not a style of leadership that necessarily produces followers. In the most stereotypical cases, prophets' actions might just as well be done on their days off.

Nevertheless, the prophet is a tempting model for social justice ministry. It is, moreover, the model many of us learn in seminary. We are well trained in many ways to be communicators, so this aspect of prophetic ministry comes naturally. We are also trained to think broadly and deeply about injustice, seeking root causes and systemic solutions and thus become like prophets who are known for their ability to think hard and cast visions. Finally, seminary prepares us to become the ones whose voices are listened to. Seminary formation tends to produce leaders who are set apart by virtue of distinctive knowledge and skills and thus ready to stand alone on issues whether others join them or not.

PRIESTLINESS

While prophecy is characterized by *speaking out*, priestliness might best be characterized by *standing with*. It is a ministry of presence. The priestly role is traditionally one of nurture and the care of souls. The priest offers succor and comfort, support and healing, through the sacraments and through ordinary gestures and presence. Inhabiting this role, a pastor presides over the rituals of the church where the sacred meets the human condition. The priest seeks to enter the lives of others and to stand with them on holy ground. This requires sensitive understanding of the human condition and a willingness to be with people, often when they are at their most vulnerable. The priestly role is one of solidarity, especially with those who are suffering.

Priestliness is often exclusively associated with its private expressions. We think of one-on-one pastoral care or spiritual direction offered within a congregation. The importance of being *present* to people is interpreted as being with them in *private*. Standing with someone on sacred ground becomes standing with them on private ground. Many who are drawn by temperament to a priestly role are often drawn into such one-on-one activities.

But priestliness is also a form of public ministry. Clergy in the priestly role may be present with those who are marginalized. They may accompany those who are hurting from injustice, taking on their burdens and suffering alongside them as witnesses. A local pastor acting in the priestly role might be the one in our scenario who hangs out with the workers in the grocery store parking lot in the mornings. (In fact, I know of a group that got pulled into local deportation policy because they had been handing out coffee to day laborers.) One thinks of the way clergy have offered sanctuary and a safe haven for others or absolution to those in need of redemption. I think of the many clergy who have, through their parishes, extended hospitality to refugees and homeless people and others who are in some way displaced and forgotten. I am reminded of a pastor who went to court with a parishioner facing sentencing after having been convicted of a crime, the pastor making a plea to the judge for a just and merciful sentence. Others have administered quietly and tirelessly to the needs of those living with addictions, standing up for the right of all to have their suffering alleviated regardless of how it came about. Still others have left home and traveled to distant and dangerous places, such as border crossings, to make a public witness on behalf of those who would otherwise face danger all alone. Some clergy work within the prison system to minister to the incarcerated or enter military zones to accompany soldiers. These are all forms of priestly ministry exercised as presence in the public realm.

The priestly role offers a complement to the prophetic role because it is less about speaking out on behalf of others and more about standing alongside them. The main problem I see with the priestly role is the way it typically gets cast as an apolitical one. For one thing, priestliness tends only to be associated with work undertaken within the fold of the congregation, not out there in public. The pastor is supposed to be present to her own flock. Second, priestliness tends to be associated with neutrality: even on matters within the congregation, the priest is not supposed to take a stand. Too often I hear the ministry of presence described in terms of what the minister should *not* do: You should not alienate anyone in your congregation. You should not disturb the pastoral bond you have forged with individuals by pushing them too hard. In order to be perceived as available to all, you should not take sides with anyone in particular. You should try to understand where everyone is coming from and not dishonor their potential need for your supportive presence. You should care for all and not express partiality. But when a matter arises that inevitably disturbs some members of the flock, neutrality leaves you with little to do. You are faced with the seeming choice between standing with your people as individuals and distancing yourself from all of them.

I think this is why pastors worry that by participating in public ministry, they will lose their credibility in the priestly role. The implication is that the priestly role demands neutrality on political issues and this may be forfeited if one takes a stand. But I also strongly suspect that the concept of a ministry of presence was not originally constructed to imply solely private interactions. The concept may have shrunk in its meaning. The ministry of presence needs to be deconstructed so that *presence* can mean standing with those who urgently need support and advocacy. Sometimes it means prodding your own flock toward movement on behalf of others.[5]

A second problem with the typical priestly role is the way it gets contrasted with the prophetic role. The former is seen as making allowance for the latter. So long as you have attended sufficiently to pastoral care, you can "get away with" being an occasional prophet. The two roles are pitted against each other rather than being seen as complementary. I once heard a pastor frame his prophetic role as something he had "purchased" at the price of his pastoral care. "I know which side my bread is buttered on," he admitted, and by this he meant all the pastoral care work he did. It kept him in the good graces of his flock and permitted him his prophetic activity as a minister. I suspect that the priestly and prophetic roles have grown apart in this unfortunate way and need not be so bifurcated. Both are complemented, after all, by a third role.

REGENCY

Jesus also ministered as a king. To be sure, during his life he rejected the title. "You say that I am," he replied, to Pilate's charge that he was claiming to be the "King of the Jews" (John 18:37). But tradition recognizes Jesus as a king not only in his victory and power over death but also in his earthly ministry. Popular understandings of royalty do not particularly help us. Too often we think of kings and queens as simply the figureheads of the state. They do not really do very much besides keep up traditions. They show up during times of pomp and circumstance. Their rule is more about appearances than about actions. Or they rule over others by demanding loyalty. But regency can be understood another way. Jesus was no ordinary king. He did not rule by domination. He did not subject people to himself. Instead, he gathered people around him and empowered them, especially his band of disciples.

To be a king, therefore, is not just to rule over subjects but, more broadly, to stir them up: to cajole, to initiate. It is to bring people together in an organized fashion and lead them somewhere. Royal ministry—or regency—then, is a public ministry style characterized by action. It is not solitary action, however; nor is it activism of the sort that can be done on a day off. A king is no one without a kingdom, and this form of public ministry is the one most dedicated to building community. The king helps the community decide what action to take and to take it together. Pastors-as-kings are charged not to be the conscience or witness or supporter of their communities but to be leaders who gather other leaders. They lead the way in developing strong relationships of solidarity that will form the basis of collective action.

While prophetic ministry is quintessentially characterized by speaking out, regent ministry begins with listening. It is an active listening, however, with probing and questioning and searching for the passion beneath the words. It is listening that builds relationship. Then the leader, connected by shared motives, moves the other to action. Regency involves agitation, in the best sense of the word. Inspired by the Spirit, this ministry is about movement and change. A famous agitator once said that action is like oxygen, animating a body of people.[6] Another metaphor for this style of ministry might therefore be *oxygenator*.

This kind of ministry also takes risks and is characterized by ingenuity and creativity. The regent is unafraid of compromise, is willing to strike deals, and is skilled at crafting policy that will work for all. It can be in this sense the most *public* form of public ministry. Those who inhabit this ministerial role must be comfortable with the rough and tumble of public life. They must develop, to a certain extent, thick skins, healthy egos, and appetites for action. Understood this way, the regency metaphor for exercising public ministry offers a way out of the prophetic-pastoral dilemma that so often blocks clergy participation in public ministry.

With these models and metaphors of public ministry resonating in our minds, let us now turn our attention to three choices you will face as you develop as a leader in public ministry. Anyone in public ministry has to decide whether to direct their energy into large, overarching problems or smaller, concrete issues. They must decide how pragmatic they are willing to be in order to effect change. They must figure out whether they can adopt a shared leadership approach with members in their community. Decisions in these three areas are not easy and involve theological as well as practical and personal considerations.

Problems versus Issues

The first choice I will discuss is that between committing your time and energy to organizations that are identified with solving big, complex problems and those working on local, concentrated issues. *Problems* include things like poverty, immigration reform, health care reform, and so on. By *issues*, in contrast, I mean things like a local living wage campaign, a municipal identification card, or a medical translation program in local hospitals.

Problems and issues are interrelated, of course, but you can tell when a group or individual is primarily working on one or the other. Groups focused on problems usually get created when disparate individuals or organizations who do not already know one another feel moved to come together around something of shared but general concern. An example from my own past might be the nuclear resistance group that formed on my college campus during the days when nuclear proliferation was grabbing headlines nationally. I joined because, like so many of my peers, I wanted to *do something* about this problem. Issue-based campaigns, in contrast, tend to start when an already-related group of people identify an injustice that affects them directly and that they can imagine changing. An example might be when an ecumenical clergy group in town joins an effort to pressure local tomato growers to pay the tomato pickers in their county a higher wage. Obviously, the contrast I have drawn is a rough one; people who don't know each other join forces around issues and tight-knit groups devote themselves to problems. Problems like nuclear proliferation can certainly have a direct effect on activists, and issues like farmworker justice can become widespread and complex. There is also a big difference between single issue groups and groups that embrace multiple issues. But the general distinction between problems and issues is still important and presents choices both practical and theological for you if you get involved.

In community organizing terms, problems are vast, eternal, general, universal, and complex. Despite this (or because of this, depending on your viewpoint), they compel you by their merit. Issues, in contrast, are manageable, winnable, specific, local, and clear. They compel you because you have an interest at stake in them. Influenced as I am by the world of community organizing, where targeting issues is always the goal, the way I have stated the differences may seem inordinately to favor the latter. And, indeed, implicit in my discussion will be a preference for devoting as much if not more of your time to local issues. But doing both kinds of justice work has advantages, both practical and theological. You need to consider where you best belong and what fits your calling.

When a problem is vast, it means that it affects a lot of people. Poverty, for example, is clearly a vast reality in the United States. It is no coincidence that organizations committed to ending poverty frequently seek to galvanize people's attention by citing statistics such as the percentage of households across the country receiving an income level below the poverty line. Such statistics are compelling, because being confronted by the widespread nature of any problem makes it harder to ignore. It is understandable that many people of faith are drawn toward large problems like ending poverty, for they cannot turn a blind eye to injustices that affect so many citizens in their society (including, sometimes, themselves). The needs generated by poverty are great, and palpable, and many in the churches cannot imagine *not* responding. At the same time, however, the very vastness of problems like ending poverty can have one of two negative effects on their activists.

On the one hand is the psychological and spiritual fatigue that can overcome those who dedicate years of time and energy to big problems only to become discouraged because these problems constantly overwhelm and sometimes seem only to get worse. My own experience in college as an antinuclear activist, for example, confirmed for me that since ridding the world of nuclear weapons was obviously too big a goal for our little campus group, what we were left with were awareness events and letters to our congresspeople, which felt to me endlessly insufficient. Even combining our numbers with other groups at marches on Washington was not enough to sustain my energy for the work, as inspiring and uplifting as those marches could be. I eventually became involved in a different campus group, one focused on the issue of a need-blind admissions and financial aid policy at our school. Persuading college administrators to maintain their commitment to this policy felt to me like a more attainable goal and was thus more satisfying to me.

On the other hand, vast problems can also have the curious effect of making activists feel satisfied even while getting done little of immediate substance. Everyone's shared problem becomes no one's problem in particular, but everyone was galvanized for a moment. My own progressive denomination is famous for gathering in biennial meetings to pass resolutions on problems like eliminating nuclear weapons, genocides, and diseases. Delegates leave the meetings affirmed in their resolve to become more aware of and dedicated to these problems. Ultimately, however, the resolutions for which we all raise our voting cards sometimes lack a sufficient mandate for any specific group or office within the denomination. It can become difficult to tell who should be held accountable for follow-through, and, sadly, sometimes very little of a concrete nature ever gets done. The proposing of resolutions does not cease, however, because awareness of and dedication to the world's problems feel like such worthy and important goals to which any self-respecting denomination should aspire.

In addition to being vast, problems never really go away. They are eternal. They both last a long time and also resurface on a regular basis. They are like the perennials of the justice world. "The poor you shall always have with you" may be an oft-misquoted line of Scripture, but the sentiment beneath it rings true to the experience of many. Reaching any lasting achievement or meaningful solution to a major problem can feel impossibly out of reach. Anyone choosing a form of public ministry devoted to a large societal problem has to be comfortable with hanging in for the long haul. *And this may be exactly the calling for some.* The opposite of an eternal problem, after all, is a short-term and winnable issue. Short-term, winnable issues may simply seem to fall too short of the mark. In the area of economic justice, for example, there are those whose goal is to end poverty in America and others who work to raise the minimum wage for discrete groups of employees in their towns. Is the latter "enough"? There may be something just too *small* about injustices that can be overcome! Indeed, some argue persuasively that Christians are not called to win issues. Too many in the secular world think too small and too much about winning, they say. Christians must be the ones to keep the eternal picture in view, even the ones to insist on striving for achievements they know to be impossible in their own lifetimes. They are to uphold an eschatological vision and commit themselves to a time frame known only to God. Anything less is to compromise Christian hope.

My point is that different theologies support different forms of public ministry. Your theology of justice may mean that you must commit yourself to causes no matter how large they are in scope. Furthermore, it may be that your formation in ministry has encouraged you in this direction. My experience is that theologies supporting faith-based activism on problems of injustice are prominent in the curricula of theological schools. The liberation theologies I studied in divinity school, for example, taught me to identify systems of oppression affecting whole classes of people. There is something in the nature of seminary that students go there to have their horizons expanded and to learn to think big. Students understandably emerge from their years in theological education filled with conviction about the necessity of looking to the root problems behind social injustices. Correspondingly, they often naturally feel that the right thing to do in their ministries is to be themselves engaged in, and get their communities engaged in, systemic approaches to eradicating injustice. Nothing is wrong with this. Equally valid, however, are theologies that support incremental steps toward justice and even the importance of winning. These theologies lift up the importance of human agency in shaping the world immediately around us. Let me give an example.

Several years ago Lutheran pastor Scott Kershner wrote in the *Christian Century* about his local church's campaign in Brooklyn, New York, to get the city to install a speed hump on the street running between the church and its parochial school buildings. Both children and adults frequently had to cross that street during the course of the day, and the speed of traffic coursing down it was dangerous. When church members gathered together to talk about the injustices in their life that they faced in common as members of St. Stephen's and citizens of Brooklyn, they could not easily find an issue until Pastor Kershner asked, "How many people think traffic moves too fast on Newkirk Avenue?" and almost everybody raised a hand. What developed out of the small group gatherings was a campaign over several months to get a speed hump in place. It took several attempts not only to identify the proper public officials who could make this happen but also to develop the most effective approaches to winning their support. Eventually the parishioners called a public meeting to which they invited several officials, after having ascertained that a commitment to speed humps was most likely in hand. Parishioners did most of the talking in the meeting, securing at the end brief yes responses from the invitees. "Each [official] was given two minutes to speak. All three spoke as if making Newkirk Avenue safer had been their idea all along, belying the bureaucratic indifference we had pushed against every step of the way. But that was OK with us. We knew better. We knew who made this happen."[7]

Several theological values were expressed in this admittedly small victory in one Brooklyn neighborhood. One was the relationship building that both allowed for and developed out of organizing for a speed hump. Church folk who may or may not have shared an experience of larger oppression could come together around children's safety and the need for traffic calming. In addition, by choosing one specific issue for the group to tackle, undoubtedly some temporarily set aside their own interests for the interests of the whole. They could feel confident that next time others would be there for them when an issue more directly affecting their own interest was at stake. Moreover, they could learn to recognize and call forth in each other the resources necessary to change something in their public life together. They could then cultivate together the virtues of forbearance and courage necessary to stand up to indifferent public officials. They learned that ultimately it was not public officials who changed communities for the better, anyway, but the grit and determination of regular folks like themselves. This is power at its best. They increasingly saw themselves as political actors capable of taking on even bigger issues. "As the organization grows, we have become better equipped to address broader policy concerns. However, whatever we taken on, we will never stray far from the skills used and lessons learned in acquiring our little speed hump. Organizing stubbornly insists that all human beings can be agents in shaping their world, whether one wants slower traffic in the neighborhood or immigration reform for the country."[8]

Returning to the differences between problems and issues, problems are further characterized by universality and complexity. One of the reasons that it can be relatively easy to win people's support for problems of injustice is that many people in many places can identify with them. They are universally recognizable and legitimate in people's eyes. There are also, however, few specifically identifiable actual targets. While it may be tempting for some of us to blame presidents or CEOs for the world's problems, it is actually quite difficult to put a face on one person responsible, say, for global warming. For this reason, it may ironically be *easier* for some of us to take a stand on global warming than it would be to stand up for a speed hump. In contrast, issues tend to be specific to locale and may not be as universally recognized as urgent and important. The local nature of issues does make it easier, relatively speaking, to identify and target those who should be held accountable. Compared to global warming, it is easier to find out who it is in your neighborhood that can get a speed hump installed. However, this also means that the targets of local issues know who is targeting them. There is a closer relationship. Putting a wildlife foundation bumper sticker on your car may not get you into trouble the way pinning your council president in a public meeting might.

Complexity means that a problem always has many facets. National policies like health care and immigration reform are examples. As soon as you wade into one of these problems by becoming at all active in it, its complexities usually become quite evident. The strategies some organizations take do not, however, reflect this complexity. They ask relatively simple responses of people. "Come to a rally at the capitol for health care reform." "On your way out of church, sign the petition against torture." "Join the Wednesday noon witness for peace." In contrast, those who approach justice work more through issues are willing to pick the facets apart and concentrate on one at a time. They start with research and proceed through to a series of actions. The strategies are as concrete as the goals sought.

When community organizers talk about the process of honing in on a particular winnable issue that represents one part of a larger problem, they talk about "cutting an issue." The image is apt. To win necessitates cutting something big into small, manageable pieces. You are likely able to imagine the pros and cons of this choice in public ministry. On the one hand, cutting an issue can feel like reducing a difficult problem down to something overly simple, in a way that fails to do it justice. The winnable issue around which you finally succeed can be so limited as to feel dissatisfactory; some in your group may have even forgotten about it. One of my students wrote about his experience in an organization that had been working for years to get medical translation services in Connecticut hospitals for those who do not speak English: "This summer I have learned that it is of the utmost importance to have throw-down parties for every mini-issue victory in order to keep both the morale of the organization high and the sanity of the leaders intact."[9] He was implying that small wins can feel unsatisfactory unless leaders build them up. But his observation also confirms the importance even of "mini-issues." Some people are in fact quite satisfied to take things one step at a time. They find their morale and sanity sustained by the process of carefully researching a problem, identifying the part of it that can be clearly and persuasively presented in public, and taking the time to organize people around it before attempting an action that might lead to victory. For them, it is frustrating constantly to circle around large problems and get nowhere.

The choice between tackling large, complex problems and winning on small, concrete issues was well described by another one of my students who interned for a summer with a congregational-based organizing group. This group was working to support the city's effort to institute a municipal identification card that would be available to all residents regardless of immigration status. Immigration, he wrote, is a multi-faceted puzzle, incorporating questions of legality, morality, law enforcement, economics, and ethnicity. . . . Rather than attempt to solve the entire problem at once, the City of New Haven cut an issue: the resident ID card. The idea does not address "amnesty," border control, exploitation of labor, the ethics of land ownership, among many, many other things. It offers safety and a sense of community. The modest steps of providing photo ID to simplify signing up for a bank account, and offering city services to residents of the city were not enough for some; but those steps were winnable and manageable. Many have responded, "It doesn't solve the problem of immigration," but that was never the goal.[10]

A final contrast between problems and issues raises yet another decision for clergy who would decide how to be involved in public life. The two are different when it comes to the theological question of self-interest. Is it all right to act on one's own behalf? Issues present themselves when we reflect on our own self-interest, after all, while problems call to us because they have merit beyond our own self-interest. It is legitimate for people of faith to throw their energies into solving problems that are not, and never may become, their own. The protest of US Christians and others against the apartheid regime in South Africa, for example, was vitally important. It was important even apart from any possible connections between South African apartheid and life in the United States. Activism on behalf of gays and lesbians by the straight community is important. Sometimes such battles simply compel us, whether or not winning them directly serves our own interests. One of the things communities of faith do is fight those battles on the sheer merit of the justice to be gained for others. At the same time, self-interest is also a legitimate starting point for justice work. Space does not allow me a thorough discussion of the role self-interest plays in faith and in public life, but community

organizers have long urged us not to discount it. Self-interest
is not the same as selfishness. People act on the interests they
have at stake, and so it is legitimate for a minister to gather people around and probe them for what they care about, the way
Pastor Kershner did when he asked, "How many people think
traffic moves too fast on Newkirk Avenue?" In the end, many
would argue that our interests ultimately ignite our passions
and therefore move us to take action. Neither is self-interest
always the same as caring about material gains. Your interests
include your values and aspirations.[11]

I believe it was Reinhold Niebuhr who said that sometimes
Christians need to "sacrifice their sacrifice." The admonition
pokes gentle fun at the preference many liberal Christians have
to act on their faith through the big gestures—conscientious
objection, civil disobedience, hunger strikes. But it is also a way
of saying that, as important as self-sacrifice is to the Christian
narrative, it is not the only theme. We may not always be called
to sacrifice ourselves for others. Sacrificial actions, after all, can
sometimes be a source of smugness. So can aligning ourselves
with ideological causes that have great moment and import. By
extension, therefore, we can interpret this piece of Niebuhrian
advice to mean that some ministers might legitimately choose
not to take on the huge problems of the day as they seek to become more active in the public realm. Small wins in the public
arena may feel to some to be inordinately self-interested, but
when looked at another way, so too can striving for the end of
never-ending problems. Local issues may strike you and your
congregation as parochial and, if so, you may need to stretch
yourselves by connecting with problems that have a more universal scope. But local issues do allow you to collaborate closely
with others on matters of shared concern. They have an imme-
diacy and intimacy that can be a source of strength even if they
do not show tremendous results. In the end, all ministers have
to decide what kind of public matters they want to engage and
to engage them with integrity.

Ideology versus Pragmatism

In addition to deciding what sort of organization to be involved with in public life, you will have to wrestle with decisions about *how* you should go about working toward the change you want. Your actions have to take place in the world as it is, even while you are trying to bring about the world as it should be. The world as it should be is our ideal. It is the kingdom of God, the realm that we hope to see realized here on earth. It is the world where God's values are not compromised and love reigns. In the world as it should be, all are committed to the common good they share. Unity and justice characterize human relationships. In the world as it should be, crossing streets with traffic is not dangerous and all have affordable health insurance.

When you choose to become involved in public life, and the time comes when you and others must take concrete action, you may have to decide how much you are willing to compromise your ideal vision in order to get something done. This is not the same decision as deciding how to cut an issue from a problem, by the way. An issue is not necessarily arrived at through compromise but rather through the process of hewing down a problem to something manageable. However, issues can then force as many if not more compromises than problems do. The reason is that they are so concrete and immediate. Problems are never ending and therefore can, in a certain way, allow you to maintain your ideology above the fray of messy issues. Issues, in contrast, usually prompt you to make a choice between ideology and pragmatism, if only because they are so concrete.

Becoming pragmatic is particularly difficult for many of us in the ministry whose education and training have formed us into people committed to an ideological vision of the good. Pragmatism, with its commitment to achieving the limited good that is possible in a given context, may utterly disappoint those who are used to preaching and teaching about the kingdom of God. Most of us spend a great deal of time becoming prepared to argue for our vision of the world as it should be. We study theories and theologies of what it looks like. We then step into pulpits and positions of leadership and try to outline our vision. We should not necessarily stop doing this. However, inevitably the time comes when we have to act, and our point of origin for acting is not the world as it should be but rather the world at hand. And there, in that world, things are a mess. Unfortunately, in the world as it is, we may ironically find that purity of vision can be as much a hindrance as an aid. As one organizer puts it, "In short, the moment you decide to act in public around a specific, tangible, concrete issue, rather than a vague chat or discussion group about a problem, you are in a world of trouble. You can't get out of it. You can only learn how to negotiate in it; deal with conflict and controversy in it; and decide how you will act with adversaries, since you can't wish them or pray them away."[12]

We are generally unable to embody our ideologies, our visions of the way the world ought to be, without making compromises. Compromise comes in many forms. You will probably find that you can rarely get the meaningful change you want without upsetting somebody, meaning that your actions will appear controversial. Meaningful change from the way things are to the way they should be almost inevitably involves taking sides, and this means you will probably be charged with bias. Leaders sometimes initially feel, in other words, that they have to compromise some of their popularity. They discover that they cannot please everyone and may have to forfeit their sense of themselves as universally likeable, genial people. Compromise may also mean having to play by the rules somebody else established, at least at first. It can mean accepting a limited amount of change—often the most difficult thing for an idealist to accept. Finally, sometimes we have to compromise our idealistic sense of right and wrong, as when we have to strike deals, form alliances with parties with whom we disagree on other matters, seek support from people who are controversial or problematic, or use less than ideal means to achieve the greater good. When actions in the world leave us tainted by compromise, ethicists call this the problem of "dirty hands." What they mean by that is when we get down to work on a problem in public life, we inevitably get into the mess it has created. We take onto our own hands some of the dirt that we have to work with. Sometimes we even find ourselves implicated in the very mess we are trying to solve.

Much more could be said about the choice between ideology and pragmatism in public life, and its associated compromises, than I have space for. Let me say just a word or two, then, a final example. Many ministers new to public life find themselves having to go up against adversaries who are not thoroughly evil and may even cause sympathy.

You may not like calling them enemies or even adversaries, but in trying to effect change in the world as it is, there will almost always be specific people that you have to counter or "do battle" with. They are the people who, at least for the time being, stand in the way of change, whose interests are aligned opposite to yours. As the organizer I quoted on the previous page said, you can only decide "how you will act with adversaries, since you can't wish them or pray them away."

Just as defense attorneys sometimes wish in vain for the perfect client, only to be disappointed by the actual flawed human being they have to represent, so too public leaders sometimes wish they had a purely evil adversary who would be easy to attack, rather than the often sympathetic characters they have to oppose. Rarely do we hate our enemies. Sometimes we even like them. Often they have done good things as well as bad things for our communities. For example, the college administrators we went up against, as students concerned about our institution's admissions policy, were generally respected individuals whose record we did not necessarily dispute when it came to other campus matters. Similarly, your members of

Congress or mayors or bishops may represent your interests on some matters and not on others. They are not always the bums we relish getting thrown out. Organizers are fond of reminding leaders that "there are no permanent enemies and no permanent allies." Just because someone's interests oppose yours on one particular issue does not mean they will be your opponent forever. Tomorrow, you may look to them as your ally on another issue. So, too, there are rarely *pure* enemies and *pure* allies. Unless you happen to encounter a thoroughly evil antagonist, you will more likely find yourself up against an ordinary human being toward whom you wish no harm.[13] Let me give an example taken from the broad-based organization of churches I knew in Connecticut.

Leaders of Elm City Congregations Organized (ECCO) in New Haven, Connecticut, like to tell the story of their founding issue, because it was a clear win with a lasting impact. But it is also the story of defeating a less than clearly bad adversary. When church members from a particular New Haven neighborhood gathered in each other's homes to talk about the changes they would like to see in their community, the issue that eventually surfaced was their children's safety at school recess. It turned out that many people's kids could not go outside at recess because they were being harassed by men who congregated around the liquor store just across the street from the playground. Many attempts ensued to get the men away from the children, all to no avail. The owner of the liquor store, though sympathetic, could not do anything. Eventually the neighbors realized that as long as there were liquor stores near playgrounds, children would be at risk. Therefore, they mounted a campaign with the city aldermen to pass an ordinance on the location of liquor stores in the city. The ordinance stipulated that all liquor stores must be located at least five hundred yards from public schools. It passed. The children got to go outdoors again for recess. Many people were very proud of what they had accomplished, and to this day, the ordinance they got passed is known as the ECCO law.

However, the owner of the liquor store lost his license and was forced out of business. He had done nothing himself to harass schoolchildren, and he was not doing anything illegal or immoral by operating his store. His was a small, locally owned business and he himself was a legal immigrant who worked hard to support himself and his family. While some members of ECCO may have been ideologically opposed to the selling of liquor, most were not. It had not been their aim to punish the store owner. Nevertheless, he and his store became the adversary in their desire to protect their children. This is an example of achieving a greater good by doing some harm to an individual who was not necessarily guilty.

All leaders have to make difficult decisions. My point here is that in public life you can sometimes wait forever to have the "perfect" adversary whose actions and motivations are so obviously bad as to be an unambiguous threat that justifies your actions. In the meantime, you may have to decide how to act toward adversaries who may even arouse your sympathies yet who stand in the way of the world as it should be.

Doing for Others versus Letting Them Do for Themselves

One thing that you may have been thinking, reading the examples of public ministry I have given, is this: left to your own devices, you may not have chosen to commit your time and energy to speed humps or school recess. Even if you agree with the importance of local issues over global problems, you still may not have selected *those* local issues. In the situations I have described, the leaders had to accept the results of the community's discernment about what most mattered to them. When you gather folks together in the church parlor to talk about their lives, it could even turn out that what matters most to them is something you consider trivial or selfish. If you choose any model of leadership in public life other than that of the utterly detached prophet, you will have to decide how much control you are really ready to give up.

Organizers have a maxim about leading others that they call the Iron Rule (dubbed this because it is a twist on the Golden Rule) that goes like this: "Never do for others what they can do for themselves." That is, leaders *can't* just be left to their own devices. As simple as this rule may sound, however, following it is not necessarily easy.

Three things make the Iron Rule hard. The first is learning to value and create space for relationship building. Building relationships starts with talking less and listening more. Clergy in particular often find they have to learn how to do this because staying quiet does not always come naturally! But seriously, I think many potential leaders assume that leadership is about finding their voice and expressing it. However, I once heard someone say that if you observe two people having a conversation, you can tell who the leader is because he or she is doing *less* of the talking.

If you are a leader following the Iron Rule, you help people build relationships with each other, not just with you. Taking a relational approach to social justice work means starting *not* with volunteer recruitment strategies or motivational speeches or example-setting actions but rather with a campaign of one-on-one conversations (called "one-on-ones" or individual meetings). As members of the community, you meet in pairs to get to know one another and form relationships before you ever take any action together. Specifically, you meet to learn each other's story. "What brings you into this work for change in the community?" you might ask, "What things do you care about, and what is it about your life that has led you to care about them?" and (for the especially bold), "What are you willing to do to get the things you care about?" Everybody has a story behind why they are moved to get involved in public life, but are so rarely invited to tell it. Taking the time to learn each other's stories builds solidarity. People don't just become more familiar with each other and with the cause but also probe and prod each other for a commitment. Relationship building increases accountability, distributes power, and keeps people engaged. Most important, this sort of intentional conversation makes people committed to each other, not just to the cause or to its leaders.

One-on-one meetings are complemented by what organizers call house meetings where members of the community come together in groups to discern what it is they want to work on together. People listen to each other and give voice to their concerns. They brainstorm ideas, identify their most pressing issues, and figure out what research they need to do and what action might be necessary to win on those issues.

Taking the time to build relationships through listening is too rarely recognized as part of justice work. Many leaders just want to recruit you for action. I know that I have gone to plenty of meetings over the years about one social justice concern or another, only to sit and listen to presentations or pleas from the leaders and then be asked to sign my name to a sheet of paper passed around the table at the end, before going home. Perhaps the leaders take the time to go around the room and ask you for your name. They may even ask you to say something brief about what brought you to the meeting. But too often these exercises feel like mere preliminaries to the real agenda of the meeting, which is to communicate the problem or issue to you and get you on board with it. If you are like me, you leave such meetings genuinely interested in the causes, having liked the presentations, even having agreed with the strategies proposed, and despite all this, find that you don't attend again. I think the reason is that you were not asked to engage with anyone else at the meeting. You were simply asked to engage with the idea and the action plan. But this is not enough for many of us. Such meetings too often represent missed opportunities for relationship, and relationship is what fuels our commitment.

Let me give an example of a missed opportunity for conversation and relationship building that I once witnessed. Ironically, the opportunity was missed despite the fact (as I learned later) that the leader's goal was to step aside and not do for others what they could do for themselves! It was an organizational meeting for an annual community project. Those who agreed to volunteer, it was explained, would be working very closely with each other for a period of time, focusing on issues that were potentially sensitive. The leader even said something about how past participants had had a very moving experience working together. But he did not so much as ask anyone at the meeting to say his or her name. He proceeded almost right away to outline the tasks as he saw them and then asked people to sign up. After the meeting, I started to express my dismay to someone else in attendance, only to discover that she thought the leader had done a very good job. The previous year's leader had taken on too much, she said, but this one had successfully delegated responsibility. It struck me in that moment that delegation is so often mistaken for effective leadership. Delegating tasks is important, but insufficient. This meeting—and, indeed, the entire project—might have garnered high marks for efficiency and management, but the leader controlled it and did not empower others to become leaders themselves. I could not help but imagine what effect members of the group might have had on the project if they had been allowed input.

We should not underestimate the leadership work that goes into helping people build relationship. For one thing, people in churches tend not to be used to meetings not wholly oriented toward the agenda and its business items. They tend to think the point is to show up and cover the items on the agenda as quickly as possible so as to keep the meeting short. The idea of including time for intentional one-on-one conversation is likely to be new. It will probably take concerted effort on the pastor's part to introduce the notion of individual or group conversation that is neither chitchat nor business nor topical discussion but rather the intentional sharing of personal stories.

The second thing that is hard about following the Iron Rule is developing the discipline of stepping aside to let others do for themselves. Community organizers are not, of course, the only ones who have discovered how important this is. Recently I ran across the concept of a ministry of encouragement that struck me as sharing many of the same features as organizing. In *Becoming Barnabas: The Ministry of Encouragement,* United Methodist pastor Paul Moots writes about the process by which he and his church completely changed the way they organized their work within the church and in the community. "The ministry of encouragement," he writes, "moves the pastor or pastoral staff out of the center of a church's ministry. More accurately, it makes room for lay leaders to join the pastor and staff in the center and to share their power, responsibility, gifts, and insight."[14]

Following a model inspired by the early Christian church in Antioch as told in the book of Acts, Moots's church, the First United Methodist Church in Mount Sterling, Ohio, revised the way they undertook all program ministries. First they started simply but powerfully with prayer. As pastor, Moots asked several people to join him in prayer for the ministries of the church and how they might be developed. He preached for one year through the book of Acts and asked people to compare its vision of church with their own reality. Then several Sunday afternoon gatherings were convened to surface members' hopes for what they wanted to see the church be and do. "I listened for those who wanted to see First Church extend its ministry to the community, for those who were dreaming of new possibilities, even for those who were dissatisfied but could not express a solid reason for their discontent."[15] Several discoveries came out of these meetings: Too few people were shouldering the burden of leadership. Too little of substance was actually getting done. For too much of their recent history there was too little partnership. Eventually First Church decided to suspend for one full year their entire committee structure and ways of doing business. Instead, they instituted a council on lay ministries to oversee new ministries that people suggested. Anyone who had an idea for a ministry was free to develop it; they did not have to be a member of the requisite committee. No cumbersome committee structure would delay implementation. Anyone could be recruited as a volunteer. The council would pray over, provide support for, and help publicize the idea.

First Church people came forth with all sorts of new projects and programs. They implemented a process for welcoming visitors. They began a tutoring program in the elementary school. They purchased a church van, began a young adult ministry, expanded a Bible study, started a community center, and more. Of all these new initiatives, Moots avers that he himself was never the driving force. "While I lent support to all of these, I initiated none of them. I did not and do not meet with any of the support committees, other than the worship team, except by invitation. Rather, these ministries were developed through the imagination and commitment of individual lay members and the council for lay ministries after a process of prayer and attentiveness to the Spirit."[16]

Pastor Moots's experience represents a remarkable example of a minister following the Iron Rule, and following it for a sustained period of time. He learned to step aside and not let his leadership dominate. He would not do for others what they could do for themselves—which in this case was to identify, plan, and carry out program ministries of the church as well as ecumenical initiatives within the wider community. This opened the way for the laity to exercise their own leadership based on their own ideas of what direction they wanted the church's ministries to take. They started from the ground up. As with community organizing, the whole process began and continued with listening sessions (and prayer) during which an expanded number of voices were heard. As he put it, "Clergy are often handed (and often seek) responsibilities that are not truly their own. They often are given an authority over the ministry of the church that limits the ideas and participation of others. If all Christ's ministers, clergy and lay, are going to use fully the gifts of the Spirit and to fulfill their individual ministries, clergy must be 'laid aside' from control of ministry so that the Spirit may call and be heard by all."[17]

It is far from easy to be "laid aside." Sometimes I think that the Iron Rule is readily embraced in theory without considering the personal and practical challenges involved. First is the question of how you really feel giving up control. I would suspect that giving it up is not easy for many of us who are formed to be ministers. In fact, Moots admits that he felt discomforted by the idea that he might not be necessary to the ministries of the church. "How dare they manage ministry without me!" he confessed to feeling at times.[18] And to make matters worse, the feeling of not really doing his job was exacerbated by the laypeople who concurred in thinking that he was not really doing his job! After all, the revolution in ministry leadership that took place at First Church was not necessarily welcomed by all, nor are other attempts at shared leadership. Some people cannot embrace the idea that ministers will exempt themselves from decision making and other kinds of control. They see this as abdicating one's role. Therefore it takes a strong ego and a lot of patience to let yourself be set aside and make yourself not do for others.

Finally, the third thing that makes following the Iron Rule hard is even if you agree that you should not do for others what they can do for themselves, and you are willing and able to relinquish the power of having your hand in everything, this does not answer the question of whether there are some things that others *cannot* do for themselves. The Iron Rule does not, after all, tell you to do nothing! Early in my own ministerial career, I made the mistake of thinking that empowering others meant simply doing less myself. I did not realize that there is still tremendous leadership work to be done when you are a leader. This is especially true for ministry in public life.

For example, Moots never suggests that all the listening and prayer that took place at First Church happened all by itself. He not only had to model it but also had to build confidence in it. As pastor, Moots formed a select group of leaders to be in conversation with him at first. This grew organically to include more people, but my point is that Moots hardly sat back to watch events unfold. In addition, my brief summary of what happened may have obscured the fact that an entire year was spent in preaching and prayer before any proposal for change went to the church at large.

Another thing it means to be a leader is to be the one who pays special attention to the practices a community adopts and who keeps those practices alive. The pastor of one church I know introduced the idea of starting every committee meeting of the church with brief individual meetings. It was exciting and felt like such an important change in culture that soon church members were bragging to people in other churches about this practice. In truth, however, after a few years the practice flagged and had to be resuscitated. The pastor's role was to keep encouraging people. Pastors also have key roles to play in articulating a common vision, presenting new possibilities, and opening doors for other potential leaders who would otherwise be overlooked. Moving the leader out of the center does not mean the leader has nothing to do. The ministry of encouragement is leadership in and of itself.

Conclusion

I return, finally, to the scenario with which I opened this chapter. I could see two ways this scenario might get played out. On the one hand, you might attend the meeting to which the Roman Catholic priest invited you and find that the others who have shown up consist of all the "usual suspects"—the activist priests, the town radicals, the known liberals. Everyone expresses horror at what has happened; the rhetoric heats up. Some start making rather long speeches, recalling times in the past when the religious community took a real stand against injustices and pleading that it be so again. Your colleague brings the discussion to order, and he asks the group to think about what they could do and come to another meeting the next week. Some want to take immediately to the streets in a protest against the chief of police. Others want nothing short of a reformed national immigration policy and urge the group to become a chapter of a larger group. Nothing is settled. You leave the meeting and remember that one of your denominational executives whom you know has studied the problem of immigration policy, so you call her for some advice. She sends you a stack of white papers and resolutions that have been written by the denomination in recent years, but the material is all directed toward what a comprehensive national policy should be, and nothing in the documents tells you what you can do specifically and immediately about a possible case of deportation in your town.

On the other hand, you might attend the meeting and find it energizing to be in the same room with so many of your clergy colleagues, united around a common interest. Everyone has shown up, from the Pentecostals to the Unitarians. Introductions are made, and it becomes clear that the ground has been laid ahead of time by many individual conversations like the one you had with your Roman Catholic colleague. Everyone has been personally invited to the meeting and, consequently, everyone feels welcome and their participation respected. The meeting begins with one-on-ones, and you develop a sense of why others have come. One person has already secured the help of some lawyers and law professors who have experience in deportation cases. The conversation focuses on everyone's common interest: the immediate tasks of figuring out how to find out where the arrested men may have been taken and providing assistance to their wives and children in the days ahead. Some agree to research possible long-term responses to the role of the town's police in deportation, but most of the time is spent on what to do during the next week. Leaders tell some stories of similar raids in other states and how they were resolved, and bring the meeting to a close.

Will you become a prophet, a priest, or a king in your public ministry? Will you combine something of each of these roles? Will you be one who takes stands, stands with, or gets others to move the stands from one place to another? Will you do more speaking or listening? Will you strive for impartiality or solidarity? Will you tackle big things or figure out what small things you can win? All of these questions and more will face you as you develop into a leader in public life. Courage in the journey!

Notes

Introduction

1. Walter Brueggemann, foreword to *Equipping the Saints: Best Practices in Contextual Theological Education*, ed. David O. Jenkins and P. Alice Rogers (Cleveland: Pilgrim Press, 2010), xiv.

2. Malcolm Gladwell, *Outliers: The Story of Success* (New York: Little, Brown, 2008), 268.

3. Daniel F. Chambliss, "The Mundanity of Excellence: An Ethnographic Report on Stratification and Olympic Swimmers," *Sociological Theory* 7, no. 1 (1989): 78.

4. Ibid., 81.

5. Ibid., 85.

Chapter 1: Are You Daniel or King Belshazzar?

1. An earlier version of this material appeared in *Equipping the Saints: Best Practices in Contextual Theological Education*, ed. David O. Jenkins and P. Alice Rogers (Cleveland: Pilgrim Press, 2010). Permission to reproduce granted.

2. M. Craig Barnes, "The Meandering Ministry," in *From Midterms to Ministry: Practical Theologians on Pastoral Beginnings*, ed. Allan Hugh Cole Jr. (Grand Rapids: William B. Eerdmans, 2008), 104.

3.   Po Bronson, "How *Not* to Talk to Your Kids: The Inverse Power of Praise," *New York Magazine*, February 19, 2007, with additional reporting by Ashley Merryman. See also Claudia S. Mueller and Carol S. Dweck, "Praise for Intelligence Can Undermine Children's Motivation and Performance," *Journal of Personality and Social Psychology* 75, no. 1 (1998): 33–52, and Carol S. Dweck, *Mindset: The New Psychology of Success* (New York: Random House, 2006), ch. 1.

4.   Dweck, *Mindset*, 170.

5.   Ibid., 4.

6.   Ibid., 46.

7.   There are three things a mindset is not necessarily correlated with. The first is achievement. Both those with fixed mindsets and those with growth mindsets achieve success; they just differ as to their motivations for achievement and the ends they seek. The fixed mindset will seek proof of given capacities while the growth mindset will seek uncharted gains. Second, confidence: someone with a fixed mindset may be very confident; it is just that their confidence is ultimately bound to be fragile. Third, accurate self-assessment. A growth mindset should *not* be equated with the belief that "I can do anything if I just try hard enough." People who have it don't inflate their own sense of what they can do. In fact, when tested, they appear to have a more accurate sense of how they rank than those with a fixed mindset. Their self-esteem is not tied to their current ranking, so they are able to be frank with themselves about how well or poorly they are doing.

8.   Bronson, "How *Not* to Talk to Your Kids," 83.

9.   Ibid.

10.   In one of the most creative requests for feedback I encountered, one of my students told his supervisor that he wanted to lead Bible study the way Jon Stewart led *The Daily Show*. The supervisor had never watched the show, but said he would check it out so that the two of them could deepen their conversation about what it means to study the Bible.

11.   See Alfie Kohn, *Punished by Reward: The Trouble with Gold Stars, Incentive Plans, A's, Praise, and Other Bribes* (New York: Houghton Mifflin, 1993), and Richard Farson and Ralph Keyes, "The Failure Tolerant Leader," *Harvard Business Review*, August 2002.

Chapter 2: Maybe She's Born with It; Maybe It's Mentoring

1.   Daniel F. Chambliss, "The Mundanity of Excellence: An Ethnographic Report on Stratification and Olympic Swimmers," *Sociological Theory* 7, no. 1 (1989): 75.

2. Brian A. Williams, *The Potter's Rib: Mentoring for Pastoral Formation* (Vancouver, BC: Regent College, 2005), 58.

3. Wallace M. Alston Jr., "What a Minister Is to Do," in *From Midterms to Ministry: Practical Theologians on Pastoral Beginnings*, ed. Allan Hugh Cole Jr. (Grand Rapids: William B. Eerdmans, 2008), 250.

4. L. Gregory Jones and Susan Pendleton Jones, "Leadership, Pastoral Identity, and Friendship," in Cole, *From Midterms to Ministry*, 25.

5. Ibid., 23–24.

6. *So You Think You Can Dance*, season 7, episode aired August 2010 (Los Angeles: Fox Broadcasting).

7. Walter C. Wright Jr., *Mentoring: The Promise of Relational Leadership* (Milton Keynes, UK: Paternoster Press, 2004), 97.

8. Williams, *Potter's Rib*, 69.

9. *Up in the Air*, directed by Jason Reitman (Hollywood: Paramount Pictures, 2009).

10. Williams, *Potter's Rib.*, 55.

11. Cleophus J. LaRue, "From Texas Pastor to Princeton Professor," in Cole, *From Midterms to Ministry*, 143.

12. Wright, *Mentoring*, 51.

13. Ibid.

14. Ibid., 45.

15. William H. Willimon, "Leaders Stay Young," *Leading Ideas* (July 7, 2010): 2, Lewis Center for Church Leadership, www.churchleadership.com. This article is adapted from his commencement address delivered at Wesley Theological Seminary, Washington, D.C., on May 10, 2010 (emphasis added). Used by permission.

16. Ibid., 1.

17. Ibid., 2.

18. "Pilot," *Numb3rs*, directed by Mick Jackson, aired January 23, 2005 (Culver City, CA: CBS Paramount Network Television).

19. Susan Fox, "Coaching Conversations," in *Reflective Practice: Formation and Supervision in Ministry* 27 (2007): 102–3.

20. David T. Gortner and John Dreibelbis, "Mentoring Clergy for Effective Leadership," in *Reflective Practice: Formation and Supervision in Ministry* 27 (2007): 64.

21. Regina Coll, *Supervision of Ministry Students* (Collegeville, MN: Liturgical Press, 1992), 23–24, ellipses in original.

22. Gortner and Dreibelbis, "Mentoring Clergy," 75, 82n23. They cite Mihaly Csikszentmihalyi, who called these behaviors "experiences of tor-mentors."

23. Coll, *Supervision of Ministry Students*, 28.

24. Ibid., 29.

25. Ibid., 60.
26. Gortner and Dreibelbis, "Mentoring Clergy," 66.
27. Ibid., 67.
28. Ibid., 70.
29. Ibid., 73.
30. Ibid., 67.
31. Williams, *Potter's Rib*, 77–78.

Chapter 3: Heads above Water: Peer Group Learning

1. Lee S. Shulman, "Teaching as Community Property: Putting an End to Pedagogical Solitude," in *The Wisdom of Practice: Essays on Teaching, Learning, and Learning to Teach*, ed. Suzanne M. Wilson (San Francisco: Jossey-Bass, 2004), 455.

2. Michael Cunningham, "A Writer Should Always Feel Like He's in Over His Head," O, *The Oprah Magazine*, July 2009, 124–25, http://www.oprah.com/omagazine/Michael-Cunningham-on-Writing/3.

3. Richard Lischer, *Open Secrets: A Spiritual Journey through a Country Church* (New York: Doubleday, 2001), 170.

4. Shulman, "Teaching as Community Property," 457.

5. Richard L. Hester and Kelli Walker-Jones, *Know Your Story and Lead with It: The Power of Narrative in Clergy Leadership* (Herndon, VA: Alban Institute, 2009), 6.

6. John A. Berntsen, *Cross-Shaped Leadership: On the Rough and Tumble of Parish Practice* (Herndon, VA: Alban Institute, 2008), 60.

7. Tim Dolan, "Making Sense of Ministry: A Clergy Cluster Project," in *A Lifelong Call to Learn: Continuing Education for Religious Leaders*, ed. D. Bruce Roberts and Robert E. Reber (Herndon, VA: Alban Institute, 2010), 170.

8. D. Bruce Roberts, "Energizing, Supporting, and Sustaining Religious Leaders through Peer Learning Groups," in Roberts and Reber, *A Lifelong Call*, 148.

9. Cunningham, "A Writer Should Always," 125.

10. Richard M. Gula, *Ethics in Pastoral Ministry* (New York: Paulist Press, 1996), 70–71.

11. Barbara J. Blodgett, *Lives Entrusted: An Ethic of Trust for Ministry* (Minneapolis: Fortress Press, 2008), 145.

12. John Wimmer, quoted in Hester and Walker-Jones, *Know Your Story*, 131.

13. Dolan, "Making Sense of Ministry," 172.

14. Hester and Walker-Jones, *Know Your Story*, 25.
15. Ibid., 3.
16. See James P. Wind and David J. Wood, *Becoming a Pastor: Reflections on the Transition into Ministry* (Herndon, VA: An Alban Institute Special Report, 2008), 14 (emphasis added).
17. Donald A. Schon, *The Reflective Practitioner: How Professionals Think in Action* (New York: Basic Books, 1983), 54.
18. Etienne Wenger, Richard McDermott, William M. Snyder, *Cultivating Communities of Practice: A Guide to Managing Knowledge* (Boston: Harvard Business School Press, 2002), 4.
19. Ibid., 8.
20. Ibid., 9.
21. Ibid., 11–12.
22. Ibid., 30–31.
23. Ibid., 46.
24. Shulman, "Teaching as Community Property," 476.
25. Ibid.
26. Ibid., 477.
27. Wind and Wood, *Becoming a Pastor*, 13–17.
28. Shulman, "Teaching as Community Property," 496.
29. Wenger et al., *Cultivating Communities of Practice*, 9.

Chapter 4: Community Property: Peer Group Practice

1. Etienne Wenger, Richard McDermott, William M. Snyder, *Cultivating Communities of Practice: A Guide to Managing Knowledge* (Boston: Harvard Business School Press, 2002), 64. See their discussion of domain, community, and practice (45–47).
2. Ibid., 85.
3. Ibid.
4. Edward T. Chambers, *Roots for Radicals: Organizing for Power, Action, and Justice* (New York: Continuum, 2004), 49.
5. Richard L. Hester and Kelli Walker-Jones, *Know Your Story and Lead with It: The Power of Narrative in Clergy Leadership* (Herndon, VA: Alban Institute, 2009), 117.
6. Ibid., 23.
7. Ibid., 26.
8. Philip Clayton in collaboration with Tripp Fuller, *Transforming Christian Theology for Church and Society* (Minneapolis: Fortress Press, 2010), 80–81.
9. Ibid., 81–82.

10. Chambers, *Roots for Radicals*, 50.

11. Alan Neely, "Case Studies as a Pedagogical and Learning Tool," *Journal for Case Teaching*, no. 11 (Fall 2000): x.

12. Sue Zabel, "Case Writing and Teaching in a Seminary: Reflecting on Ministry Experience," unpublished material from the Association for Case Teaching, Abilene, TX.

13. Hester and Walker-Jones, *Know Your Story*, 36.

14. Ibid., 35.

15. Roy M. Oswald, *Clergy Self-Care: Finding a Balance for Effective Ministry* (Herndon, VA: Alban Institute, 1991), 138.

16. Ibid., 131. Oswald cites the following source: Bruce Reed, The Oscillation Theory from *The Task of the Church and the Role of Its Members* (Herndon, VA: Alban Institute, 1975).

17. Oswald, *Clergy Self-Care*, 137.

18. See Penny Long Marler, "Peer Groups Matter: The Impact of Leadership, Composition, and Cost," in *A Lifelong Call to Learn: Continuing Education for Religious Leaders*, ed. D. Bruce Roberts and Robert E. Reber (Herndon, VA: Alban Institute, 2010), 103–5.

19. For this insight I am indebted to the monthly book discussion group of the Society for the Advancement of Continuing Education for Ministry, a peer group I currently belong to.

20. Penny Long Marler, "Peer Groups Matter," 113–14.

21. Tim Dolan, "Making Sense of Ministry," in Roberts and Reber, *Lifelong Call to Learn*, 167.

22. See Wenger et al., *Cultivating Communities of Practice*, 109–111.

Chapter 5: Prophet, Priest, or King?

1. Gaylord Noyce, *Pastoral Ethics: Professional Responsibilities of the Clergy* (Nashville: Abingdon Press, 1988), 151.

2. Edward T. Chambers, *Roots for Radicals: Organizing for Power, Action, and Justice* (New York: Continuum, 2004), 30.

3. Noyce, *Pastoral Ethics*, 151.

4. Ibid., 152–53.

5. I am indebted here to Ryan Eller, a Baptist pastor and the Lead Community Organizer for CHANGE (Communities Helping All Neighbors Gain Empowerment) in Winston-Salem, North Carolina.

6. Saul Alinsky, "Action is to the organization as oxygen is to the body," quoted in Chambers, *Roots for Radicals*, 80.

7. Scott Kershner, "Speed Hump Victory," *Christian Century*, May 20, 2008, 13. Used by permission.

8. Ibid.

9. Jonah Bartlett, final paper for "Leadership in Public Ministry," Yale Divinity School, Summer 2008. Used by permission.

10. Kevin Luy, final paper for "Leadership in Public Ministry," Yale Divinity School, Summer 2008. Used by permission.

11. David Carter, e-mail communication with author, July 13, 2010.

12. Patrick Speer, "The Theology under ECCO" (training document, Elm City Congregations Organized, July 2006). Used by permission.

13. As I write this, the US public is coming to terms with the extent of a catastrophic oil spill in the Gulf of Mexico. The CEO of British Petroleum has become the face of this catastrophe, and he is widely reviled. Rarely is one person so closely identified with a problem, however, and even in this case it could be argued that there are other "enemies," including those who opposed tighter government regulation of the oil industry.

14. Paul Moots, *Becoming Barnabas: The Ministry of Encouragement* (Herndon, VA: Alban Institute, 2004), 4.

15. Ibid., 16.

16. Ibid., 23.

17. Ibid., 29.

18. Ibid., 31.